PENGUIN PLAYS
FOUR AMERICAN PLAYS

FOUR AMERICAN PLAYS

WITH AN INTRODUCTION BY
CHARLES MAROWITZ

EDWARD ALBEE
THE AMERICAN DREAM

JACK RICHARDSON
GALLOWS HUMOUR

MURRAY SCHISGAL
THE TYPISTS

ARTHUR MILLER
INCIDENT AT VICHY

PENGUIN BOOKS
In association with Jonathan Cape and Martin Secker & Warburg

Penguin Books Ltd, Harmondsworth, Middlesex, England
Penguin Books, 40 West 23rd Street, New York, New York 10010, U.S.A.
Penguin Books Australia Ltd, Ringwood, Victoria, Australia
Penguin Books Canada Ltd, 2801 John Street, Markham, Ontario, Canada L3R 1B4
Penguin Books (N.Z.) Ltd, 182–190 Wairau Road, Auckland 10, New Zealand

—

The American Dream
First published in the U S A. 1961
Published in Great Britain by Jonathan Cape 1962
Copyright © Edward Albee, 1960, 1961

Gallows Humour
First published in the U.S.A. by Dutton 1961
Copyright © Jack C. Richardson, 1961

The Typists
First published in the U.S.A. 1963
Published in Great Britain by Jonathan Cape, 1964
Copyright © Murray Schisgal, 1963

Incident at Vichy
First published in the U.S.A. 1965
Published in Great Britain by Martin Secker & Warburg 1966
Copyright © Arthur Miller, as an unpublished play
Copyright © Arthur Miller, 1965

This collection first published in Penguin Books as *New American Drama* 1966
Reprinted 1970, 1973, 1976, 1978
Reprinted as *Four American Plays* 1982, 1985

This collection copyright © Penguin Books, 1966
Introduction copyright © Charles Marowitz, 1966
All rights reserved

—

Made and printed in Great Britain by
Richard Clay (The Chaucer Press) Ltd,
Bungay, Suffolk
Set in Monotype Garamond

CONTENTS

INTRODUCTION

PERHAPS the most significant fact about the plays in this collection is that none of them originated on Broadway. Three were first presented in off-Broadway theatres, and the fourth in a subsidized cultural complex specifically designed as an alternative to Broadway.

For years now, it has been generally acknowledged that Broadway is dying. The serious magazines have lashed it regularly, and even the faithful Times Square set have become rancorous. The death of an institution as glamorous as Broadway is certainly something to be mourned, but in the midst of diatribes and lamentations, what has been overlooked is that Broadway was not only dying in itself, but killing everything around it. One might muster sympathy for a cancer-victim, but when the sufferer is infected with bubonic plague, all one can honourably do is flee the scene. This, to a large extent, is what has happened. Some of the best theatre people defected (even if only a few streets downtown) and others found greener pastures outside of New York. The decline of Broadway coincided with a civic theatre boom, and, with support from organizations like the Ford and Rockefeller foundations, first-class professional theatres sprang up in cities like Dallas, New Orleans, Minneapolis, Denver, Washington and San Francisco.

Although Broadway likes to pretend its problem is fundamentally economic (an impasse created by high production costs and grasping trade unions), the real rot is artistic. But of course, economics and aesthetics invariably intertwine. Broadway is no longer in the hands of anyone even remotely connected with the theatre. The dim, pot-bellied producers of old were, at least nominally, in the theatre. But as time went on and prices got higher, they started being dictated to by the realtors who owned the theatres and hankered after 'sure fire hits'. Now even they are no longer in control. The new trend-setters are the 'fat ladies in fancy hats' who organize theatre parties and guarantee six or more months of block bookings if the fare is suitably cosy and mindless. Broadway has become an adjunct of big business. It caters to the business community to whom theatre tickets are an item on a corporation expense-account. A 'show' has become an elaborately extended gin-and-tonic used to break down the resistance of out-of-town buyers. (Hence the relatively new genre of musicals and comedies that glorify the business-ethic: *Come Blow Your Horn, Seidman and Son, I Can Get It For You Wholesale, How to Succeed in Business Without Really Trying*, etc.) Offerings that can be guaranteed to divert are at a premium. Plays that 'disturb' or 'make you think' are to be shunned. The Broadway dictum is very simple: art soothes, anything that doesn't soothe is, by definition, anti-art.

The fact that musicals and comedies proliferate doesn't necessarily dictate the ruin of the theatre, but it has become harder and harder to maintain the high standards of the past. As for the so-called 'legit' offerings, they have become distressingly attenuated. The musicals are, at least, gay, bouncy and professional, and on occasion the comedies have been fleet and funny. But the straight drama has remained in the clammy clutches of Strasberg (né Freud), which is to say, psychological realism as a dramatic style, and faithfully observed behaviourism as an acting style. The assumption underlying this style is that art equals verisimilitude, and so long as Freudian postulates can corroborate human behaviour, the plays in which such behaviour occurs are taken as 'true'. Motivation is insisted upon by the writers as much as by the actors. The resultant drama is prescribed, explicit, logically progressive, socially convincing, morally simplex, and profoundly unsatisfying.

The source of the dissatisfaction with this kind of theatre was that, in spite of the verisimilitude, life simply wasn't like that. Reality contained more mansions than the psychological. At the heart of experience was not a well-diagnosed behaviour-pattern, but mystery. Its ultimate point and purpose could not be summed up in a few pat phrases, but was something so contradictory and ambiguous that to try to state it at all was to topple into simplification. But this drama prospered, supported by its traditional props: big moments, violent passions, animal-magnetism, heart, hoopla, pace, buncombe, schmaltz, fraud.

What the 'new drama' did was to re-define reality – or rather widen the definition then in vogue. Beckett and Ionesco, two very different writers, whose characteristics are blurred rather than clarified by labels like Theatre of the Absurd, revealed a world founded on nihilism and absurdity. To some Americans, a world without logic (Ionesco's) might just as well be a world without God; and a world without God (Beckett's) was positively subversive. But the moods of these plays were in keeping with the generations of the fifties and sixties, the people who had seen political idealism devoured by the war, and Christianity reduced to the level of a parlour joke by existentialist philosophy. And while Beckett and Ionesco shot holes in the carefully ordered worlds of the social-dramatists, Jean Genet, carrying subversion even further, painted a picture of life heavily tinted with private fantasy and filled with rituals that went deeper than obsessional neuroses. Beckett and Ionesco merely passed a cynical judgement on organized society, Genet refused to believe it existed at all, except as an elaborate, staunchly held illusion. And so in three swipes, and within the space of seven years, a drama rooted in the tangible and the verifiable was nudged in the direction of the metaphysical. Needless to say, there were many who resented the nudging.

The best of the American playwrights in the forties and fifties had been critical of society; of the way people behaved towards each other or the way power-groups behaved towards the individual. It was a room-sized drama where writers like Lillian Hellman, William Inge, Arthur Miller and Tennessee Williams squeezed at middle-class pimples. The implicit theme for all these writers was social behaviour. The new continental playwrights on the other hand dealt directly with *existence* as a subject in itself, and consequently dealt with it philosophically. Of course, it was still *people* and *social behaviour*, but the frame of reference was no longer sociological. What made all this relevant was the fact that the world had almost blown itself up, and philosophic speculation was going on in the minds of ordinary people to a much greater extent than ever before. In the twenties people talked real estate and booze; in the thirties the key words were 'organize' and 'planned society'; in the forties the lid blew off, and after World War Two – the revelations of the concentration camps, the unrelieved cold-war tensions – the great preoccupation was with life itself. How long would we live? How long before the bomb? It wasn't so much that the drama was 'new'. The consciousness of ourselves had become new and, quite naturally, it looked for confirmation in art, just as it inevitably found expression there.

But the curious thing in America was that the new writers, ostensibly influenced by Beckett, Ionesco, Genet, etc., only adopted the stylistic traits of these writers, not their metaphysical inclination, and what followed was a 'new' drama that was 'new' only in stylistic terms. Those unbreakable 'old' American 'bottles' took away much of the flavour of all that imported 'new wine'.

In America, no matter which political party is in office, the national compulsion is towards conformity. One feels it everywhere – in the clothes, the houses, the air-conditioning units, the coke-bottles and, of course, the values. In the New Frontier, the old and honourable ideal of rugged individualism was no longer possible (the only real routes to individualism were social rebellion or criminality – which may account for the fact that these are so often mixed up). And so, the new idealism centred around Protest. The marches, the demonstrations, the sit-ins, the identification with civil rights' movements – all of this was a physical alternative to sameness. Protest in America has almost become a new orthodoxy. It is the distinguishing mark of the new singers, the new comedians, the new writers. It infiltrates theatre-vernacular. Robert Brustein's muscle-bound academic tome is called *The Theatre of Revolt*, Herbert Blau's book *The Impossible Theatre* is subtitled 'a manifesto'. Le Roi Jones, the freshest new American playwright, 'wants blood'. Norman Mailer is calling for 'a revolution of sensibility'. It is not so much that Americans are living in revolutionary times, but rather that they are in a period when conformity is so overpowering they must have the pretence of protest to make their lives bearable at all.

In such a national context, any writer who takes up an aggressive stance – like Edward Albee – automatically takes on an exaggerated importance. *Who's Afraid of Virginia Woolf?* is a generalized social indictment, and it is this very generality that so weakens its case. Its psychological tensions are real enough; its political attitude, assumed and unconvincing. (First-class up-dated Strindberg perhaps, but very bogus Ibsen.) A play like THE AMERICAN DREAM, overtly social and satiric, reveals more about the author's private mythology than it does about the society he is ostensibly attacking. The fact that the sub-text of the play is Ionesco's *The Bald Prima Donna*, and that its invective owes something to the caustic exchanges of Estragon and Vladimir, is irrelevant. One doesn't fault the play because it slides conveniently into an Absurdist sea, but because once there, it doesn't sail under its own steam. However, the play is full of marginal virtues. It beautifully captures the accents of contemporary American speech – not only the easy vernacular, but the thought-patterns, the motives, the inanities of the language. The character of Grandma is out of the rock-solid tradition of the American wisecracker, and goes to town beautifully on the treasured hypocrisies of old-age, infirmity and death – a lovable old broad with pincers in her teeth.

But in merely stating his main character and not developing him, Albee loses a marvellous opportunity for satire. The strikingly handsome, appallingly vapid All-American Boy is a peculiarly American tragedy. Jack Armstrong, the well-adjusted Wheaties-eater, is both comic and tragic within his social context, but it isn't enough simply to have him introduce himself. When we see him admired by his elders (what a clean-cut fella), courted by women (what a dreamboat), idealized by his pals (a great guy!) and wooed by the big-industry boys (he'll go far, that one), we tend to forget that he is a fatuous, hollow, football-toting, orgiastic primitive. No play has really done a proper job on him, although he has turned up in unlikely works such as *Tea and Sympathy* (by inference) and *Death of a Salesman* (brawny, vapid, Happy Loman).

The American Dream itself is like a marvellous dancer that never leaves the spot. It is static in an atmosphere of movement. Although broadly conceived, it doesn't move broadly and so, at the end, one finds oneself liking it for things it *should* have said, and is almost deceived into thinking it *has* said them.

Where Albee uses social imagery to disguise personal problems, Jack Richardson heads straight for the social points, using personal situations diagrammatically, to illustrate the comment. He is the most English of the American playwrights, using language consciously, even classically, unashamedly employing conceits, flourishes and rhetoric. What is so effective in GALLOWS HUMOUR is that the play doesn't tackle conformity merely as a concept, a large, generalized evil, but as a particularly nauseating form of human repression. The tight, white collar of the suburban commuter carried to its logical, metaphorical conclusion is the noose, and in each of Richardson's two acts, it is the sense of physical constriction which in one case liberates, in the other oppresses, his heroes.

When I directed this play at the Traverse Theatre in Edinburgh, my main worry was how to convey the blackness of this black comedy without letting an audience off the hook with laughter. I hasten to point out that the play is wildly funny and intended to be, but in the coda of each act the situation tightens up (like a noose) and turns into a tart, moral indictment. My frets about balancing up the farce-comedy with what one might call socially oriented Grand Guignol were uncalled for, because the mechanics of the play are so perfect, it changes gear automatically. And, as we proved by switching interpretations during the course of the run, this shift of emphasis occurs in spite of changed intentions on the part of actors. Which I take to be a compliment to the play's structure.

But just as one admired *Gallows Humour* as a piece of stage-craft, one couldn't help noting its light-weightedness. The play is too pat. It gives off no repercussions. It says what it sets out to say and no more, and what it sets out to say is too limited. It lacks those clinging ambiguities that make a play tempting to come back to time and time again, like a really well-wrought piece of music in which one never catches everything at first hearing. But Richardson remains one of the most promising (that wretched word which shouldn't be pinned on any writer out of his teens) of the new Americans, because his style is his own, his control is masterly and his imagery is both theatrically and verbally rich. Now if he can only come up with something worth saying.

At the moment Murray Schisgal is very much the sum of his influences (Ionesco being the most pronounced), although he has certain distinguishing marks of his own. Stylistically, he is more sophisticated than Albee, and his knack of jumping time and condensing narrative enables him to get further away from naturalism than most of his contemporaries. But, originally a writer of prose, he is still sloppy in writing words to be spoken. A Schisgal play is often edited into existence, usually by other hands. The comic talent is instinctive and grows out of the cross-talk patterns of vaudeville and burlesque comedy, which gives it a very solid American foundation. The hard-core sentimentality is part of a similar, less endearing tradition.

I met Schisgal in 1960 when, as a frustrated schoolteacher and unproduced playwright, he came to London toting three thick volumes full of short plays. Of the dozens I read, I chose three which seemed viable for a triple-bill. The first two, *The Tiger* and *Simple Kind of Love Story*, were patently shorthand versions of larger ideas ('three act plays with one missing' as the *Statesman* critic observed) which, nevertheless, worked as miniatures. In fact, the dramatic shorthand method soon proved to be one of their most theatrical qualities. The plays' greatest asset, a commonplace in the cinema but never really achieved in the theatre, was speed: speed of thought conveyed through speed of action (a quality very unlike *pace*, which is too often an arbitrary acceleration of tempo). This was a narrative fleetness which managed to cover as much ground as a really well-told anecdote. The third play, THE TYPISTS, used the device more subtly, and because technique and theme happened to correspond, used it to the best effect.

The Typists is an hour-long transformation scene in which one very simple, progressive image (actors ageing before our eyes) captures the futility of life better than many ambitious, full-length plays. The relentless decrescendo of the typists' day is accompanied by all the fervent trivia which are the language of our lives, and the condensation-device registers this with savage clarity. The play conveys an almost Chekhovian sense of dulled routine and empty rituals and, like Chekov, it demonstrates the utter impossibility of acting upon profound personal perceptions which cry out for positive action. The psychoanalytic parlour game – I'll tell you what's wrong with you: You tell me what's wrong with me – is played with brutal and unflagging regularity in many American circles where a couch is a piece of psychic rather than domestic furniture. And it is this sense of being trapped in the midst of total consciousness which creates the pathos in the lives of Schisgal's typists. So far, Schisgal has distinguished himself only as a miniaturist. He has yet to write a play with flesh, rather than skin-graftings, on its bones.

The play which will seem out of place in this collection is INCIDENT AT VICHY, and it will seem so because it is; and although clever intellectual lassooing could bring the Miller play into the herd, it would be more to the point to examine the work for its differences.

Its virtues are simple and undeniable: workmanlike; builds dramatically; convincing characterizations (albeit reminiscent of B-type war films); fired with the writer's characteristic sense of conviction. What is curious about the play is that it meets all the requirements of 'good drama' and yet fails to satisfy. And the reason for this is a kind of rectitude (I almost said: self-righteousness) which burns in its centre. It has easy villains and easy heroes. The moral conflict is black and white. The 'good guy' is, of course, the man of conscience; and the bad guys are, of course, malicious people who proceed from anti-humanist principles. It is the facility of the play's moral structure which ultimately downs it. We have reached a state in the theatre (in life, I should say) when we can no longer abide questions whose answers are so clearly implied. They not only rob us of certain essential mysteries, but tempt us to suspect a playwright's fairness. And despite Miller's high reputation for justice, liberalism, etc., the play, artistically speaking, is unfair. In being so fully committed morally, it robs us of the pleasure of disentangling the rights and wrongs for ourselves. Certainly, no one is going to make a brief *for* racism and *against* tolerance, but today, one has to go much further into the enemy camp to score a victory for the 'forces of right', because so many of us are tarred with the same brush. It is this inescapable historical fact, the knowledge of our own criminality, that makes the moral pose so vulnerable.

Most contemporary plays about Nazi oppression (Hochuth's *The Representative*, Weiss's *The Investigation*, etc.) are much too loaded to convey the impartiality we unconsciously look for in a work of art. And the impartiality I am referring to does not preclude having a viewpoint and plumping for it. It doesn't mean watering down one's own moral view (although it could mean topping up the negative argument). It simply means that we are not so sold on the unquestionable rightness of our view, that we present all other views only perfunctorily.

It is in matters like this that a playwright like John Arden seems so contemporary when compared to Miller. Arden, whose plays deal with themes similar to Miller's, is never in evidence as a moral arbiter. He presents the issues, and the impartiality is sometimes so insistent that we often don't know where Arden stands: although we are never in doubt as to our own positions. There is one view of the theatre (and I subscribe to it) which claims that the business of the drama is to supply evidence, all the evidence, short of glutting the stage and boring the audience. Then by arranging the blocks of this evidence dramatically, the play engages the imagination of the audience. It is much more realistic (if realism is the desired boon) because in our own lives, the facts are not spread out before us in a set order, but have to be gleaned from conflicting accounts, persuasive counter-arguments, distortions, half-truths and lies. In short, from a great variety of evidence. Arden, out of an enormous respect for the evidence, provides as much as he can muster, and the judgement we ultimately make is all the more significant because it is *ours*, and not merely an underwriting of the playwright's. This I take to be audience participation on the highest possible level.

The growth of an individual act of conscience which dooms one man and saves another will always be a peg for a crackling good drama. But the world in which such an act emerges *must* be more complex than Miller's if it's to reflect our own.

A final word to put this collection into a larger perspective. The influences at work in all of these plays originates as far back as Ibsen and as far forward as the French existentialist upsurge of the fifties. It would be misleading to suggest that these are the only influences affecting contemporary writers in America. If we take Jack Gelber, Kenneth Brown, Le Roi Jones and the collectively devised plays of the Living Theatre as being symptomatic of the future, then the name we must end with is not Beckett, Ionesco or Genet, but Antonin Artaud.

That cruelty is the style of our times does not make us any different from the Renaissance or Jacobean age or the periods of the American Revolution, Civil War or Depression. Cruelty, like love, is always with us. But what seems clear is that some new theatre-aesthetic is forming, based on Artaud's concept of cruelty. This latter is not synonymous with blood and violence, but has more to do with a certain rigour which we apply to life and which it, likewise, applies to us. If this were a completely contemporary collection intending to suggest the *zeitgeist*, it would include the scores of several Happenings, and the improvised script of the Living Theatre's 'Frankenstein' epic. The fact that it doesn't shouldn't blind us to the fact that what is happening in America today (the underground swell as opposed to the surface fashion) is as different from the replicas of Beckett and Ionesco as the plays of Miller are from Philip Barry. If a collection like this appears in twenty years' time, I prophesy its contents will bear so little resemblance to these plays that we'll all be asking (with no little chagrin) what the hell has happened to the theatre we knew. If this prophecy is untrue, and the writers of 1985 are only slightly modified versions of Albee, Schisgal, Richardson and Miller, the American theatre will be all the poorer for it.

CHARLES MAROWITZ

EDWARD ALBEE

THE AMERICAN DREAM

A Play in One Scene (1959–1960)

For David Diamond

PREFACE

THE comments by the Messrs. Watts, Bailliett, and Taubman, while they are representative of a majority of critical reaction to *The American Dream*, do not tell the whole story. Naturally not. No sensible publisher will tout opinions antagonistic to his product. And while I have, in my brief (three years, five plays – two of them but fifteen minutes long) and happy time as a playwright, received enough good press to last me a lifetime, I would like to concern myself, here, with some of the bad – not because I am a masochist, but because I would like to point up, foolhardy though it may be of me, what I consider to be a misuse of the critical function in American press letters.

For example: the off-Broadway critic for one of New York's morning tabloids had his sensibilities (or something) so offended by the *content* of *The American Dream* that he refused to review the next play of mine that opened.

Another example: a couple of other critics (Bright Gentlemen who do their opinions for Intellectualist Weekly Sheets of – sadly, all in all – very small circulation) went all to pieces over the (to their mind) nihilist, immoral, defeatist *content* of the play. And so on.

May I submit that when a critic sets himself up as an arbiter of morality, a judge of the matter and not the manner of a work, he is no longer a critic; he is a censor.

And just what is the *content* of *The American Dream* (a comedy, yet) that so upsets these guardians of the public morality? The play is an examination of the American Scene, an attack on the substitution of artificial for real values in our society, a condemnation of complacency, cruelty, emasculation and vacuity; it is a stand against the fiction that everything in this slipping land of ours is peachy-keen.

Is the play offensive? I certainly hope so; it was my intention to offend – as well as amuse and entertain. Is it nihilist, immoral, defeatist? Well, to that let me answer that *The American Dream* is a picture of our time – as I see it, of course. Every honest work is a personal, private yowl, a statement of one individual's pleasure or pain; but I hope that *The American Dream* is something more than that. I hope that it transcends the personal and the private, and has something to do with the anguish of us all.

Edward Albee

New York City, 24 *May* 1961

First performed at the York Playhouse, New York City, 24 January 1961.

CAST

MOMMY	*Jane Hoffman*
DADDY	*John C. Becher*
GRANDMA	*Sudie Bond*
MRS BARKER	*Nancy Cushman*
THE YOUNG MAN	*Ben Piazza*

Directed by *Alan Schneider*

THE PLAYERS

MOMMY	MRS BARKER
DADDY	YOUNG MAN
GRANDMA	

Scene: A living-room. Two armchairs, one towards either side of the stage, facing each other diagonally out towards the audience. Against the rear wall, a sofa. A door, leading out from the apartment, in the rear wall, far stage right. An archway, leading to other rooms, in the side wall, stage left.

At the beginning, MOMMY *and* DADDY *are seated in the armchairs,* DADDY *in the armchair stage left,* MOMMY *in the other.*

[*Curtain up. A silence. Then:*]

MOMMY: I don't know what can be keeping them.

DADDY: They're late, naturally.

MOMMY: Of course, they're late; it never fails.

DADDY: That's the way things are today, and there's nothing you can do about it.

MOMMY: You're quite right.

DADDY: When we took this apartment, they were quick enough to have me sign the lease; they were quick enough to take my cheque for two months' rent in advance. . . .

MOMMY: And one month's security. . . .

DADDY: . . . and one month's security. They were quick enough to check my references; they were quick enough about all that. But now! But now, try to get the icebox fixed, try to get the doorbell fixed, try to get the leak in the johnny fixed! Just try it . . . they aren't so quick about *that*.

MOMMY: Of course not; it never fails. People think they can get away with anything these days . . . and, of course, they can. I went to buy a new hat yesterday. [*Pause.*] I said, I went to buy a new hat yesterday.

DADDY: Oh! Yes . . . yes.

MOMMY: Pay attention.

DADDY: I *am* paying attention, Mommy.

MOMMY: Well, be sure you do.

DADDY: Oh, I am.

MOMMY: All right, Daddy; now listen.

DADDY: I'm listening, Mommy.

MOMMY: You're sure!

DADDY: Yes . . . yes, I'm sure. I'm all ears.

MOMMY [*giggles at the thought; then*]: All right, now. I went to buy a new hat yesterday and I said, 'I'd like a new hat, please.' And so, they showed me a few hats, green ones and blue ones, and I didn't like any of them, not one bit. What did I say? What did I just say?

DADDY: You didn't like any of them, not one bit.

MOMMY: That's right; you just keep paying attention. And then they showed me one that I did like. It was a lovely little hat, and I said, 'Oh, this is a lovely little hat; I'll take this hat; oh my, it's lovely. What colour is it?' And they said, 'Why, this is beige; isn't it a lovely little beige hat?' And I said, 'Oh, it's just lovely.' And so, I bought it. [*Stops, looks at* DADDY.]

DADDY [*to show he is paying attention*]: And so you bought it.

MOMMY: And so I bought it, and I walked out of the store with the hat right on my head, and I ran spang into the chairman of our woman's club, and she said, 'Oh, my dear, isn't that a lovely little hat? Where did you get that lovely little hat? It's the loveliest little hat; I've always wanted a wheat-coloured hat *myself*.' And I said, 'Why, no, my dear; this hat is beige; beige.' And she laughed and said, 'Why no, my dear, that's a wheat-coloured hat . . . wheat. I know beige from wheat.' And I said, 'Well, my dear, I know beige from wheat, too.' What did I say? What did I just say?

DADDY [*tonelessly*]: Well, my dear, I know beige from wheat, too.

MOMMY: That's right. And she laughed, and she said, 'Well, my dear, they certainly put one over on you. That's wheat if I ever saw wheat. But it's lovely, just the same.' And then she walked off. She's a dreadful woman, you don't know her; she has dreadful taste, two dreadful children, a dreadful house, and an absolutely adorable husband who sits in a wheel chair all the time. You don't know him. You don't know anybody, do you? She's just a dreadful woman, but she *is* chairman of our woman's club, so naturally I'm terribly fond of her. So, I went right back into the hat shop, and I said, 'Look here; what do you mean selling me a hat that you say is beige, when it's wheat all the time . . . wheat! I can tell beige from wheat any day in the week, but not in this artificial light of yours.' They have artificial light, Daddy.

DADDY: Have they!

MOMMY: And I said, 'The minute I got outside I could tell that it wasn't a beige hat at all; it was a wheat hat.' And they said to me, 'How could you tell that when you had the hat on the top of your head?' Well, that made me angry, and so I made a scene right there; I screamed as hard as I could; I took my hat off and I threw it down on the counter, and oh, I made a terrible scene. I said, I made a terrible scene.

DADDY [*snapping to*]: Yes . . . yes . . . good for you!

MOMMY: And I made an absolutely terrible scene; and they became frightened, and they said, 'Oh, madam; oh, madam.' But I kept right on, and finally they admitted that they might have made a mistake; so they took my hat into the back, and then they came out again with a hat that looked exactly like it. I took one look at it, and I said, 'This hat is wheat-coloured; wheat.' Well, of course, they said, 'Oh, no, madam, this hat is beige; you go outside and see.' So, I went outside, and lo and behold, it *was* beige. So I bought it.

DADDY [*clearing his throat*]: I would imagine that it was the same hat they tried to sell you before.

MOMMY [*with a little laugh*]: Well, of course it was!

DADDY: That's the way things are today; you just can't get satisfaction; you just try.

MOMMY: Well, *I* got satisfaction.

DADDY: That's right, Mommy. *You did* get satisfaction, didn't you?

MOMMY: Why are they so late? I don't know what can be keeping them.

DADDY: I've been trying for two weeks to have the leak in the johnny fixed.

MOMMY: You can't get satisfaction; just try. *I* can get satisfaction, but you can't.

DADDY: I've been trying for two weeks and it isn't so much for my sake; I can always go to the club.

MOMMY: It isn't so much for my sake, either; I can always go shopping.

DADDY: It's really for Grandma's sake.

MOMMY: Of course it's for Grandma's sake. Grandma cries every time she goes to the johnny as it is; but now that it doesn't work it's even worse, it makes Grandma think she's getting feeble-headed.

DADDY: Grandma *is* getting feeble-headed.

MOMMY: Of course Grandma is getting feeble-headed, but not about her johnny-do's.

DADDY: No; that's true. I must have it fixed.

MOMMY: WHY are they so late? I don't know what can be keeping them.

DADDY: When they came here the first time, they were ten minutes early; they were quick enough about it then.

[*Enter* GRANDMA *from the archway, stage left. She is loaded down with boxes, large and small, neatly wrapped and tied.*]

MOMMY: Why Grandma, look at you! What *is* all that you're carrying?

GRANDMA: They're boxes. What do they look like?

MOMMY: Daddy! Look at Grandma; look at all the boxes she's carrying!

DADDY: My goodness, Grandma; look at all those boxes.

GRANDMA: Where'll I put them?

MOMMY: Heavens! I don't know. Whatever are they for?

GRANDMA: That's nobody's damn business.

MOMMY: Well, in that case, put them down next to Daddy; there.

GRANDMA [*dumping the boxes down, on and around* DADDY'S *feet*]: I sure wish you'd get the john fixed.

DADDY: Oh, I do wish they'd come and fix it. We hear you . . . for hours . . . whimpering away. . . .

MOMMY: Daddy! What a terrible thing to say to Grandma!

GRANDMA: Yeah. For shame, talking to me that way.

DADDY: I'm sorry, Grandma.

MOMMY: Daddy's sorry, Grandma.

GRANDMA: Well, all right. In that case I'll go get the rest of the boxes. I suppose I deserve being talked to that way. I've gotten so old. Most people think that when you get so old, you either freeze to death, or you burn up. But you don't. When you get so old, all that happens is that people talk to you that way.

DADDY [contrite]: I said I'm sorry, Grandma.

MOMMY: Daddy said he was sorry.

GRANDMA: Well, that's all that counts. People being sorry. Makes you feel better; gives you a sense of dignity, and that's all that's important . . . a sense of dignity. And it doesn't matter if you don't care, or not, either. You got to have a sense of dignity, even if you don't care, 'cause, if you don't have that, civilization's doomed.

MOMMY: You've been reading my book club selections again!

DADDY: How dare you read Mommy's book club selections, Grandma!

GRANDMA: Because I'm old! When you're old you gotta do something. When you get old, you can't talk to people because people snap at you. When you get so old, people talk to you that way. That's why you become deaf, so you won't be able to hear people talking to you that way. And that's why you go and hide under the covers in the big soft bed, so you won't feel the house shaking from people talking to you that way. That's why old people die, eventually. People talk to them that way. I've got to go and get the rest of the boxes. [GRANDMA exits.]

DADDY: Poor Grandma, I didn't mean to hurt her.

MOMMY: Don't you worry about it; Grandma doesn't know what she means.

DADDY: She knows what she says, though.

MOMMY: Don't you worry about it; she won't know that soon. I love Grandma.

DADDY: I love her, too. Look how nicely she wrapped these boxes.

MOMMY: Grandma has always wrapped boxes nicely. When I was a little girl, I was very poor, and Grandma was very poor, too, because Grandpa was in heaven. And every day, when I went to school, Grandma used to wrap a box for me, and I used to take it with me to school; and when it was lunchtime, all the little boys and girls used to take out their boxes of lunch, and they weren't wrapped nicely at all, and they used to open them and eat their chicken legs and chocolate cakes; and I used to say, 'Oh, look at my lovely lunch box; it's so nicely wrapped it would break my heart to open it.' And so, I wouldn't open it.

DADDY: Because it was empty.

MOMMY: Oh no. Grandma always filled it up, because she never ate the dinner she cooked the evening before; she gave me all her food for my lunch box the next day. After school, I'd take the box back to Grandma, and she'd open it and eat the chicken legs and chocolate cake that was inside. Grandma used to say, 'I love day-old cake.' That's where the expression day-old cake came from. Grandma always ate everything a day late. I used to eat all the other little boys' and girls' food at school, because they thought my lunch box was empty. They thought my lunch box was empty, and that's why I wouldn't open it. They thought I suffered from the sin of pride, and since that made them better than me, they were very generous.

DADDY: You were a very deceitful little girl.

MOMMY: We were very poor! But then I married you, Daddy, and now we're very rich.

DADDY: Grandma isn't rich.

MOMMY: No, but you've been so good to Grandma she feels rich. She doesn't know you'd like to put her in a nursing home.

DADDY: I wouldn't!

MOMMY: Well, heaven knows, *I* would! I can't stand it, watching her do the cooking and the housework, polishing the silver, moving the furniture. . . .

DADDY: She likes to do that. She says it's the least she can do to earn her keep.

MOMMY: Well, she's right. You can't live off people. I can live off you, because I married you. And aren't you lucky all I brought with me was Grandma. A lot of women I know would have brought their whole families to live off you. All I brought was Grandma. Grandma is all the family I have.

DADDY: I feel very fortunate.

MOMMY: You should. I have a right to live off of you because I married you, and because I used to let you get on top of me and bump your uglies; and I have a right to all your money when you die. And when you do, Grandma and I can live by ourselves . . . if she's still here. Unless you have her put away in a nursing home.

DADDY: I have no intention of putting her in a nursing home.

MOMMY: Well, I wish somebody would do something with her!

DADDY: At any rate, you're very well provided for.

MOMMY: You're my sweet Daddy; that's very nice.

DADDY: I love my Mommy.

[*Enter* GRANDMA *again, laden with more boxes.*]

GRANDMA [*dumping the boxes on and around* DADDY'S *feet*]: There; that's the lot of them.

DADDY: They're wrapped so nicely.

GRANDMA [*to* DADDY]: You won't get on my sweet side that way . . .

MOMMY: Grandma!

GRANDMA: . . . telling me how nicely I wrap boxes. Not after what you said: how I whimpered for hours. . . .

MOMMY: Grandma!

GRANDMA [*to* MOMMY]: Shut up! [*to* DADDY] You don't have any feelings, that's what's wrong with you. Old people make all sorts of noises, half of them they can't help. Old people whimper, and cry, and belch, and make great hollow rumbling sounds at the table; old people wake up in the middle of the night screaming, and find out they haven't even been asleep; and when old people *are* asleep, they try to wake up, and they can't . . . not for the longest time.

MOMMY: Homilies, homilies!

GRANDMA: And there's more, too.

DADDY: I'm really very sorry, Grandma.

GRANDMA: I know you are, Daddy; it's Mommy over there makes all the trouble. If you'd listened to me, you wouldn't have married her in the first place. She was a tramp and a trollop and a trull to boot, and she's no better now.

MOMMY: Grandma!

GRANDMA [*to* MOMMY]: Shut up! [*to* DADDY] When she was no more than eight years old she used to climb up on my lap and say, in a sickening little voice, 'When I gwo up, I'm going to mahwy a wich old man; I'm going to set my wittle were end right down in a tub o' butter, that's what I'm going to do.' And I warned you, Daddy; I told you to stay away from her type. I told you to. I did.

MOMMY: You stop that! You're my mother, not his!

GRANDMA: I am?

DADDY: That's right, Grandma. Mommy's right.

GRANDMA: Well, how would you expect somebody as old as I am to remember a thing like that? You don't make allowances for people. I want an allowance. I want an allowance!

DADDY: All right, Grandma; I'll see to it.

MOMMY: Grandma! I'm ashamed of you.

GRANDMA: Humf! It's a fine time to say that. You should have gotten rid of me a long time ago if that's the way you feel. You should have had Daddy set me up in business somewhere. . . . I could have gone into the fur business, or I could have been a singer. But no; not you. You wanted me around so you could sleep in my room when Daddy got fresh. But now it isn't important, because Daddy doesn't want to get fresh with you any more, and I don't blame him. You'd rather sleep with me, wouldn't you, Daddy?

MOMMY: Daddy doesn't want to sleep with anyone. Daddy's been sick.

DADDY: I've been sick. I don't even want to sleep in the apartment.

MOMMY: You see? I told you.

DADDY: I just want to get everything over with.

MOMMY: That's right. Why are they so late? Why can't they get here on time?

GRANDMA [*an owl*]: Who? Who? . . . Who? Who?

MOMMY: You know, Grandma.

GRANDMA: No, I don't.

MOMMY: Well, it doesn't really matter whether you do or not.

DADDY: Is that true?

MOMMY: Oh, more or less. Look how pretty Grandma wrapped these boxes.

GRANDMA: I didn't really like wrapping them; it hurt my fingers, and it frightened me. But it had to be done.

MOMMY: Why, Grandma?

GRANDMA: None of your damn business.

MOMMY: Go to bed.

GRANDMA: I don't want to go to bed. I just got up. I want to stay here and watch. Besides . . .

MOMMY: Go to bed.

DADDY: Let her stay up, Mommy; it isn't noon yet.

GRANDMA: I want to watch; besides . . .

DADDY: Let her watch, Mommy.

MOMMY: Well all right, you can watch; but don't you dare say a word.

GRANDMA: Old people are very good at listening; old people don't like to talk; old people have colitis and lavender perfume. Now I'm going to be quiet.

DADDY: She never mentioned she wanted to be a singer.

MOMMY: Oh, I forgot to tell you, but it was ages ago.

[*The doorbell rings.*]

Oh, goodness! Here they are!

GRANDMA: Who? Who?

MOMMY: Oh, just some people.

GRANDMA: The van people? Is it the van people? Have you finally done it? Have you called the van people to come and take me away?

DADDY: Of course not, Grandma!

GRANDMA: Oh, don't be too sure. She'd have you carted off too, if she thought she could get away with it.

MOMMY: Pay no attention to her, Daddy. [*An aside to* GRANDMA] My God, you're ungrateful!

[*The doorbell rings again.*]

DADDY [*wringing his hands*]: Oh dear; oh dear.

MOMMY [*still to* GRANDMA]: Just you wait; I'll fix your wagon. [*Now, to* DADDY] Well, go let them in Daddy. What are you waiting for?

DADDY: I think we should talk about it some more. Maybe we've been hasty . . . a little hasty, perhaps.

[*Doorbell rings again.*]

I'd like to talk about it some more.

MOMMY: There's no need. You made up your mind; you were firm; you were masculine and decisive.

DADDY: We might consider the pros and the . . .

MOMMY: I won't argue with you; it has to be done; you were right. Open the door.

DADDY: But I'm not sure that . . .

MOMMY: Open the door.

DADDY: Was I firm about it?

MOMMY: Oh, so firm; so firm.

DADDY: And was I decisive?

MOMMY: So decisive! Oh, I shivered.

DADDY: And masculine? Was I really masculine?

MOMMY: Oh, Daddy, you were so masculine; I shivered and fainted.

GRANDMA: Shivered and fainted, did she? Humf!

MOMMY: You be quiet.

GRANDMA: Old people have a right to talk to themselves; it doesn't hurt the gums, and it's comforting.

[*Doorbell rings again.*]

DADDY: I shall now open the door.

MOMMY: WHAT a masculine Daddy! Isn't he a masculine Daddy?

GRANDMA: Don't expect me to say anything. Old people are obscene.

MOMMY: Some of your opinions aren't so bad. You know that?

DADDY [*backing off from the door*]: Maybe we can send them away.

MOMMY: Oh, look at you! You're turning into jelly; you're indecisive; you're a woman.

DADDY: All right. Watch me now; I'm going to open the door. Watch. Watch!

MOMMY: We're watching; we're watching.

GRANDMA: *I'm* not.

DADDY: Watch now; it's opening. [*He opens the door.*] It's open! [MRS BARKER *steps into the room.*]

Here they are!

MOMMY: Here they are!

GRANDMA: Where?

DADDY: Come in. You're late. But, of course, we expected you to be late; we were saying that we expected you to be late.

MOMMY: Daddy, don't be rude! We were saying that you just can't get satisfaction these days, and we were talking about you, of course. Won't you come in?

MRS BARKER: Thank you. I don't mind if I do.

MOMMY: We're very glad that you're here, late as you are. You do remember us, don't you? You were here once before. I'm Mommy, and this is Daddy, and that's Grandma, doddering there in the corner.

MRS BARKER: Hello, Mommy; hello, Daddy; and hello there, Grandma.

DADDY: Now that you're here, I don't suppose you could go away and maybe come back some other time.

MRS BARKER: Oh no; we're much too efficient for that. I said hello there, Grandma.

MOMMY: Speak to them, Grandma.

GRANDMA: I don't see them.

DADDY: For shame, Grandma; they're here.

MRS BARKER: Yes, we're here, Grandma. I'm Mrs Barker. I remember you; don't you remember me?

GRANDMA: I don't recall. Maybe you were younger, or something.

MOMMY: Grandma! What a terrible thing to say!

MRS BARKER: Oh now, don't scold her, Mommy; for all she knows she may be right.

DADDY: Uh . . . Mrs Barker, is it? Won't you sit down?

MRS BARKER: I don't mind if I do.

MOMMY: Would you like a cigarette, and a drink, and would you like to cross your legs?

MRS BARKER: You forget yourself, Mommy; I'm a professional woman. But I will cross my legs.

DADDY: Yes, make yourself comfortable.

MRS BARKER: I don't mind if I do.

GRANDMA: Are they still here?

MOMMY: Be quiet, Grandma.

MRS BARKER: Oh, we're still here. My, what an unattractive apartment you have!

MOMMY: Yes, but you don't know what a trouble it is. Let me tell you . . .

DADDY: I was saying to Mommy . . .

MRS BARKER: Yes, I know. I was listening outside.

DADDY: About the icebox, and . . . the doorbell . . . and the . . .

MRS BARKER: . . . and the johnny. Yes, we're very efficient; we have to know everything in our work.

DADDY: Exactly what do you do?

MOMMY: Yes, what is your work?

MRS BARKER: Well, my dear, for one thing, I'm chairman of your woman's club.

MOMMY: Don't be ridiculous. I was talking to the chairman of my woman's club just yester–. Why, so you are. You remember, Daddy, the lady I was telling you about? The lady with the husband who sits in the *swing*? Don't you remember?

DADDY: No . . . no. . . .

MOMMY: Of course you do. I'm so sorry, Mrs Barker. I would have known you anywhere, except in this artificial light. And look! You have a hat just like the one I bought yesterday.

MRS BARKER [*with a little laugh*]: No, not really; this hat is cream.

MOMMY: Well, my dear, that may look like a cream hat to you, but I can . . .

MRS BARKER: Now, now; you seem to forget who I am.

MOMMY: Yes, I do, don't I? Are you sure you're comfortable? Won't you take off your dress?

MRS BARKER: I don't mind if I do. [*She removes her dress.*]

MOMMY: There. You must feel a great deal more comfortable.

MRS BARKER: Well, I certainly *look* a great deal more comfortable.

DADDY: I'm going to blush and giggle.

MOMMY: Daddy's going to blush and giggle.

MRS BARKER [*pulling the hem of her slip above her knees*]: You're lucky to have such a man for a husband.

MOMMY: Oh, don't I know it!

DADDY: I just blushed and giggled and went sticky wet.

MOMMY: Isn't Daddy a caution, Mrs Barker?

MRS BARKER: Maybe if I smoked . . .?

MOMMY: Oh, that isn't necessary.

MRS BARKER: I don't mind if I do.

MOMMY: No; no, don't. Really.

MRS BARKER: I don't mind . . .

MOMMY: I won't have you smoking in my house, and that's that! You're a professional woman.

DADDY: Grandma drinks AND smokes; don't you, Grandma?

GRANDMA: No.

MOMMY: Well, now, Mrs Barker; suppose you tell us why you're here.

GRANDMA [*as* MOMMY *walks through the boxes*]: The boxes . . . the boxes . . .

MOMMY: Be quiet, Grandma.

DADDY: What did you say, Grandma?

GRANDMA [*as* MOMMY *steps on several of the boxes*]: The boxes, damn it!

MRS BARKER: Boxes; she said boxes. She mentioned the boxes.

DADDY: What about the boxes, Grandma? Maybe Mrs Barker is here because of the boxes. Is that what you meant, Grandma?

GRANDMA: I don't know if that's what I meant or not. It's certainly not what I *thought* I meant.

DADDY: Grandma is of the opinion that . . .

MRS BARKER: Can we assume that the boxes are for us? I mean, can we assume that you had us come here for the boxes?

MOMMY: Are you in the habit of receiving boxes?

DADDY: A very good question.

MRS BARKER: Well, that would depend on the reason we're here. I've got my fingers in so many little pies, you know. Now, I can think of one of my little activities in which we are in the habit of receiving *baskets*; but more in a literary sense than really. We *might* receive boxes, though, under very special circumstances. I'm afraid that's the best answer I can give you.

DADDY: It's a very interesting answer.

MRS BARKER: *I* thought so. But, does it help?

MOMMY: No; I'm afraid not.

DADDY: I wonder if it might help us any if I said I feel misgivings, that I have definite qualms.

MOMMY: Where, Daddy?

DADDY: Well, mostly right here, right around where the stitches were.

MOMMY: Daddy had an operation, you know.

MRS BARKER: Oh, you poor Daddy! I didn't know; but then, how could I?

GRANDMA: You might have asked; it wouldn't have hurt you.

MOMMY: Dry up, Grandma.

GRANDMA: There you go. Letting your true feelings come out. Old people aren't dry enough, I suppose. My sacks are empty, the fluid in my eyeballs is all caked on the inside edges, my spine is made of sugar candy, I breathe ice; but you don't hear me complain. Nobody hears old people complain because people think that's all old people do. And *that's* because old people are gnarled and sagged and twisted into the shape of a complaint. [*Signs off.*] That's all.

MRS BARKER: What was wrong, Daddy?

DADDY: Well, you know how it is: the doctors took out something that was there and put in something that wasn't there. An operation.

MRS BARKER: You're very fortunate, I should say.

MOMMY: Oh, he is; he is. All his life, Daddy has wanted to be a United States Senator; but now . . . why now he's changed his mind, and for the rest of his life he's going to want to be Governor . . . it would be nearer the apartment, you know.

MRS BARKER: You *are* fortunate, Daddy.

DADDY: Yes, indeed; except that I get these qualms now and then, definite ones.

MRS BARKER: Well, it's just a matter of things settling; you're like an old house.

MOMMY: Why Daddy, thank Mrs Barker.

DADDY: Thank you.

MRS BARKER: Ambition! That's the ticket. I have a brother who's very much like you, Daddy . . . ambitious. Of course, he's a great deal younger than you; he's even younger than I am . . . if such a thing is possible. He runs a little newspaper. Just a little newspaper . . . but he runs it. He's chief cook and bottle washer of that little newspaper, which he calls *The Village Idiot*. He has such a sense of humour; he's so self-deprecating, so modest. And he'd never admit it himself, but he *is* the Village Idiot.

MOMMY: Oh, I think that's just grand. Don't you think so, Daddy?

DADDY: Yes, just grand.

MRS BARKER: My brother's a dear man, and he has a dear little wife, whom he loves, dearly. He loves her so much he just can't get a sentence out without mentioning her. He wants everybody to know he's married. He's really a stickler on that point; he can't be introduced to anybody and say hello without adding, 'Of course, I'm married.' As far as I'm concerned, he's the chief exponent of Woman Love in this whole country; he's even been written up in psychiatric journals because of it.

DADDY: Indeed!

MOMMY: Isn't that lovely.

MRS BARKER: Oh, I think so. There's too much woman hatred in this country, and that's a fact.

GRANDMA: Oh, I don't know.

MOMMY: Oh, I think that's just grand. Don't you think so, Daddy?

DADDY: Yes, just grand.

GRANDMA: In case anybody's interested . . .

MOMMY: Be quiet, Grandma.

GRANDMA: Nuts!

MOMMY: Oh, Mrs Barker, you *must* forgive Grandma. She's rural.

MRS BARKER: I don't mind if I do.

DADDY: Maybe Grandma has something to say.

MOMMY: Nonsense. Old people have nothing to say; and if old people *did* have something to say, nobody would listen to them. [*To* GRANDMA] You see? I can pull that stuff just as easy as you can.

GRANDMA: Well, you got the rhythm, but you don't really have the quality. Besides, you're middle-aged.

MOMMY: I'm proud of it!

GRANDMA: Look. I'll show you how it's really done. Middle-aged people think they can do anything, but the truth is that middle-aged people can't do most things as well as they used to. Middle-aged people think they're special because they're like everybody else. We live in the age of deformity. You see? Rhythm *and* content. You'll learn.

DADDY: I do wish I weren't surrounded by women; I'd like some men around here.

MRS BARKER: You can say that again!

GRANDMA: I don't hardly count as a woman, so can I say my piece?

MOMMY: Go on. Jabber away.

GRANDMA: It's very simple; the fact is, these boxes don't have anything to do with why this good lady is come to call. Now, if you're interested in knowing why these boxes *are* here . . .

DADDY: I'm sure that must be all very true, Grandma, but what does it have to do with why . . . pardon me, what is that name again?

MRS BARKER: Mrs Barker.

DADDY: Exactly. What does it have to do with why . . . that name again?

MRS BARKER: Mrs Barker.

DADDY: Precisely. What does it have to do with why what's-her-name is here?

MOMMY: They're here because we asked them.

MRS BARKER: Yes. That's why.

GRANDMA: Now if you're interested in knowing why these boxes *are* here . . .

MOMMY: Well, nobody *is* interested!

GRANDMA: You can be as snippety as you like for all the good it'll do you.

DADDY: You two will have to stop arguing.

MOMMY: I don't argue with her.

DADDY: It will just have to stop.

MOMMY: Well, why don't you call a van and have her taken away?

GRANDMA: Don't bother; there's no need.

DADDY: No, now, perhaps I can go away myself. . . .

MOMMY: Well, one or the other; the way things are now it's impossible. In the first place, it's too crowded in this apartment. [To GRANDMA] And it's you that takes up all the space, with your enema bottles, and your Pekinese, and God-only-knows-what-else . . . and now all these boxes. . . .

GRANDMA: These boxes are . . .

MRS BARKER: I've never heard of enema *bottles*. . . .

GRANDMA: She means enema bags, but she doesn't know the difference. Mommy comes from extremely bad stock. And besides, when Mommy was born . . . well, it was a difficult delivery, and she had a head shaped like a banana.

MOMMY: You ungrateful – Daddy? Daddy, you see how ungrateful she is after all these years, after all the things we've done for her? [To GRANDMA] One of these days you're going away in a van; that's what's going to happen to you!

GRANDMA: Do tell!

MRS BARKER: Like a banana?

GRANDMA: Yup, just like a banana.

MRS BARKER: My word!

MOMMY: You stop listening to her; she'll say anything. Just the other night she called Daddy a hedgehog.

MRS BARKER: She didn't!

GRANDMA: That's right, baby; you stick up for me.

MOMMY: I don't know where she gets the words; on the television, maybe.

MRS BARKER: Did you really call him a hedgehog?

GRANDMA: Oh look; what difference does it make whether I did or not?

DADDY: Grandma's right. Leave Grandma alone.

MOMMY [to DADDY]: How dare you!

GRANDMA: Oh, leave her alone, Daddy; the kid's all mixed up.

MOMMY: You see? I told you. It's all those television shows.

Daddy, you go right into Grandma's room and take her television and shake all the tubes loose.

DADDY: Don't mention tubes to me.

MOMMY: Oh! Mommy forgot! [*To* MRS BARKER]: Daddy has tubes now, where he used to have tracts.

MRS BARKER: Is that a fact!

GRANDMA: I know why this dear lady is here.

MOMMY: You be still.

MRS BARKER: Oh, I do wish you'd tell me.

MOMMY: No! No! That wouldn't be fair at all.

DADDY: Besides, she knows why she's here; she's here because we called them.

MRS BARKER: La! But that still leaves me puzzled. I know I'm here because you called us, but I'm such a busy girl, with this committee and that committee, and the Responsible Citizens Activities I indulge in.

MOMMY: Oh my; busy, busy.

MRS BARKER: Yes, indeed. So I'm afraid you'll have to give me some help.

MOMMY: Oh, no. No, you must be mistaken. I can't believe we asked you here to give you any help. With the way taxes are these days, and the way you can't get satisfaction in ANYTHING . . . no, I don't believe so.

DADDY: And if you need help . . . why, I should think you'd apply for a Fulbright Scholarship. . . .

MOMMY: And if not that . . . why, then a Guggenheim Fellowship. . . .

GRANDMA: Oh, come on; why not shoot the works and try for the Prix de Rome. [*Under her breath to* MOMMY *and* DADDY] Beasts!

MRS BARKER: Oh, what a jolly family. But let me think. I'm knee-deep in work these days; there's the Ladies' Auxiliary Air Raid Committee, for one thing; how do you feel about air raids?

MOMMY: Oh, I'd say we're hostile.

DADDY: Yes, definitely; we're hostile.

MRS BARKER: Then, you'll be no help there. There's too much hospitality in the world these days as it is; but I'll not badger you! There's a surfeit of badgers as well.

GRANDMA: While we're at it, there's been a run on old people, too. The Department of Agriculture, or maybe it wasn't the Department of Agriculture – anyway, it was some department that's run by a girl – put out figures showing that ninety per cent of the adult population of the country is over eighty years old . . . or eighty per cent is over ninety years old . . .

MOMMY: You're such a liar! You just finished saying that everyone is middle-aged.

GRANDMA: I'm just telling you what the government says . . . that doesn't have anything to do with what . . .

MOMMY: It's that television! Daddy, go break her television.

GRANDMA: You won't find it.

DADDY [*wearily getting up*]: If I must . . . I must.

MOMMY: And don't step on the Pekinese; it's blind.

DADDY: It may be blind, but Daddy isn't. [*He exits, through the archway, stage left.*]

GRANDMA: You won't find *it*, either.

MOMMY: Oh, I'm so fortunate to have such a husband. Just think: I could have a husband who was poor, or argumentative, or a husband who sat in a wheel chair all day. . . . OOOOHHHH! *What* have I said? What *have* I said?

GRANDMA: You said you could have a husband who sat in a wheel . . .

MOMMY: I'm mortified! I could die! I could cut my tongue out! I could . . .

MRS BARKER [*forcing a smile*]: Oh, now . . . now . . . don't think about it . . .

MOMMY: I could . . . why, I could . . .

MRS BARKER: . . . don't think about it . . . really. . . .

MOMMY: You're quite right. I won't think about it, and that way I'll forget that I ever said it, and that way it will be all right. [*Pause.*] There . . . I've forgotten. Well, now, now that Daddy is out of the room we can have some girl talk.

MRS BARKER: I'm not sure that I . . .

MOMMY: You *do* want to have some girl talk, don't you?

MRS BARKER: I was going to say I'm not sure that I wouldn't care for a glass of water. I feel a little faint.

MOMMY: Grandma, go get Mrs Barker a glass of water.

GRANDMA: Go get it yourself. I quit.

MOMMY: Grandma loves to do little things around the house; it gives her a false sense of security.

GRANDMA: I quit! I'm through!

MOMMY: Now, you be a good Grandma, or you know what will happen to you. You'll be taken away in a van.

GRANDMA: You don't frighten me. I'm too old to be frightened. Besides . . .

MOMMY: WELL! I'll tend to you later. I'll hide your teeth . . . I'll . . .

GRANDMA: Everything's hidden.

MRS BARKER: I *am* going to faint. I *am*.

MOMMY: Good heavens! I'll go myself. [*As she exits, through the archway, stage left.*] I'll fix you, Grandma. I'll take care of you later. [*She exits.*]

GRANDMA: Oh, go soak your head. [*To* MRS BARKER] Well, dearie, how do you feel?

MRS BARKER: A little better, I think. Yes, much better, thank you, Grandma.

GRANDMA: That's good.

MRS BARKER: But . . . I feel so lost . . . not knowing why I'm here . . . and, on top of it, they say I was here before.

GRANDMA: Well, you were. You weren't *here*, exactly, because we've moved around a lot, from one apartment to another, up and down the social ladder like mice, if you like similes.

MRS BARKER: I don't . . . particularly.

GRANDMA: Well, then, I'm sorry.

MRS BARKER [*suddenly*]: Grandma, I feel I can trust you.

GRANDMA: Don't be too sure; it's every man for himself around this place. . . .

MRS BARKER: Oh . . . is it? Nonetheless, I really do feel that I can trust you. *Please* tell me why they called and asked us to come. I implore you!

GRANDMA: Oh my; that feels good. It's been so long since anybody implored me. Do it again. Implore me some more.

MRS BARKER: You're your daughter's mother, all right!

GRANDMA: Oh, I don't mean to be hard. If you won't implore me, then beg me, or ask me, or entreat me . . . just anything like that.

MRS BARKER: You're a dreadful old woman!

GRANDMA: You'll understand some day. Please!

MRS BARKER: Oh, for heaven's sake! . . . I implore you . . . I beg you . . . I beseech you!

GRANDMA: Beseech! Oh, that's the nicest word I've heard in ages. You're a dear, sweet woman. . . . You . . . beseech . . . me. I can't resist that.

MRS BARKER: Well, then . . . please tell me why they asked us to come.

GRANDMA: Well, I'll give you a hint. That's the best I can do, because I'm a muddle-headed old woman. Now listen, because it's important. Once upon a time, not too very long ago, but a long enough time ago . . . oh, about twenty years ago . . . there was a man very much like Daddy, and a woman very much like Mommy, who were married to each other, very much like Mommy and Daddy are married to each other; and they lived in an apartment very much like one that's very much like this one, and they lived there with an old woman who was very much like yours truly, only younger, because it was some time ago; in fact, they were all somewhat younger.

MRS BARKER: How fascinating!

GRANDMA: Now, at the same time, there was a dear lady very much like you, only younger then, who did all sorts of Good Works. . . . And one of the Good Works this dear lady did was in something very much like a volunteer capacity for an organization very much like the Bye-Bye Adoption Service, which is near by and which was run by a terribly deaf old lady very much like the Miss Bye-Bye who runs the Bye-Bye Adoption Service near by.

MRS BARKER: How enthralling!

GRANDMA: Well, be that as it may. Nonetheless, one afternoon this man, who was very much like Daddy, and this woman who was very much like Mommy came to see this dear lady who did all the Good Works, who was very much like you, dear, and they were very sad and very hopeful, and they cried and smiled and bit their fingers, and they said all the most intimate things.

MRS BARKER: How spell-binding! What did they say?

GRANDMA: Well, it was very sweet. The woman, who was very much like Mommy, said that she and the man who was very much like Daddy had never been blessed with anything very much like a bumble of joy.

MRS BARKER: A what?

GRANDMA: A bumble; a bumble of joy.

MRS BARKER: Oh, like bundle.

GRANDMA: Well, yes; very much like it. Bundle, bumble; who cares? At any rate, the woman, who was very much like Mommy, said that they wanted a bumble of their own, but that the man, who was very much like Daddy, couldn't have a bumble; and the man, who was very much like Daddy, said that yes, they had wanted a bumble of their own, but that the woman, who was very much like Mommy, couldn't have one, and that now they wanted to buy something very much like a bumble.

MRS BARKER: How engrossing!

GRANDMA: Yes. And the dear lady, who was very much like you, said something that was very much like, 'Oh, what a shame; but take heart . . . I think we have just the bumble *for* you.' And, well, the lady, who was very much like Mommy, and the man, who was very much like Daddy, cried and smiled and bit their fingers, and said some more intimate things, which were totally irrelevant but which were pretty hot stuff, and so the dear lady, who was very much like you, and who had something very much like a penchant for pornography, listened with something very much like enthusiasm. 'Whee,' she said. 'Whoooopeeeeee!' But that's beside the point.

MRS BARKER: I suppose *so*. But how gripping!

GRANDMA: Anyway . . . they *bought* something very much like a bumble, and they took it away with them. But . . . things didn't work out very well.

MRS BARKER: You mean there was trouble?

GRANDMA: You got it. [*With a glance through the archway.*] But, I'm going to have to speed up now because I think I'm leaving soon.

MRS BARKER: Oh. Are you really?

GRANDMA: Yup.

MRS BARKER: But old people don't go anywhere; they're either taken places, or put places.

GRANDMA: Well, this old person is different. Anyway . . . things started going badly.

MRS BARKER: Oh yes. Yes.

GRANDMA: Weeeeellll . . . in the first place, it turned out the bumble didn't look like either one of its parents. That was enough of a blow, but things got worse. One night, it cried its heart out, if you can imagine such a thing.

MRS BARKER: Cried its heart out! Well!

GRANDMA: But that was only the beginning. Then it turned out it only had eyes for its Daddy.

MRS BARKER: For its Daddy! Why, any self-respecting woman would have gouged those eyes right out of its head.

GRANDMA: Well, she did. That's exactly what she did. But then, it kept its nose up in the air.

MRS BARKER: Ufggh! How disgusting!

GRANDMA: That's what they thought. But *then*, it began to develop an interest in its you-know-what.

MRS BARKER: In its you-know-what! Well! I hope they cut its hands off at the wrists!

GRANDMA: Well, yes, they did that eventually. But first, they cut of its you-know-what.

MRS BARKER: A much better idea!

GRANDMA: That's what they thought. But after they cut off its you-know-what, it *still* put its hands under the covers, *looking* for its you-know-what. So, finally, they *had* to cut off its hands at the wrists.

MRS BARKER: Naturally!

GRANDMA: And it was such a resentful bumble. Why, one day it called its Mommy a dirty name.

MRS BARKER: Well, I hope they cut its tongue out!

GRANDMA: Of course. And then, as it got bigger, they found out all sorts of terrible things about it, like: it didn't have a head on its shoulders, it had no guts, it was spineless, its feet were made of clay . . . just dreadful things.

MRS BARKER: Dreadful!

GRANDMA: So you can understand how they became discouraged.

MRS BARKER: I certainly can! And what did they do?

GRANDMA: What did they do? Well, for the last straw, it finally up and died; and you can imagine how *that* made them feel, their having paid for it, and all. So, they called up the lady who sold them the bumble in the first place and told her to come right over to their apartment. They wanted satisfaction; they wanted their money back. That's what they wanted.

MRS BARKER: My, my, my.

GRANDMA: How do you like *them* apples?

MRS BARKER: My, my, my.

DADDY [*off stage*]: Mommy! I can't find Grandma's television, and I can't find the Pekinese, either.

MOMMY [*off stage*]: Isn't that funny! And I can't find the water.

GRANDMA: Heh, heh, heh. I told them everything was hidden.

MRS BARKER: Did you hide the water, too?

GRANDMA [*puzzled*]: No. No, I didn't do *that*.

DADDY [*off stage*]: The truth of the matter is, I can't even find Grandma's room.

GRANDMA: Heh, heh, heh.

MRS BARKER: My! You certainly did hide things, didn't you?

GRANDMA: Sure, kid, sure.

MOMMY [*sticking her head in the room*]: Did you ever hear of such a thing, Grandma? Daddy can't find your television, and he can't find the Pekinese, and the truth of the matter is he can't even find your room.

GRANDMA: I told you. I hid everything.

MOMMY: Nonsense, Grandma! Just wait until I get my hands on you. You're a trouble-maker . . . that's what you are.

GRANDMA: Well, I'll be out of here pretty soon, baby.

MOMMY: Oh, you don't know how right you are! Daddy's been wanting to send you away for a long time now, but I've been restraining him. I'll tell you one thing, though . . . I'm getting sick and tired of this fighting, and I might just let him have his way. Then you'll see what'll happen. Away you'll go; in a van, too. I'll let Daddy call the van man.

GRANDMA: I'm way ahead of you.

MOMMY: How can you be so old and so smug at the same time? You have no sense of proportion.

GRANDMA: You just answered your own question.

MOMMY: Mrs Barker, I'd much rather you came into the kitchen for that glass of water, what with Grandma out here, and all.

MRS BARKER: I don't see what Grandma has to do with it; and besides, I don't think you're very polite.

MOMMY: You seem to forget that you're a guest in this house . . .

GRANDMA: Apartment!

MOMMY: Apartment! And that you're a professional woman. So, if you'll be so good as to come into the kitchen, I'll be more than happy to show you where the water is, and where the glass is, and then you can put two and two together, if you're clever enough. [*She vanishes.*]

MRS BARKER [*after a moment's consideration*]: I suppose she's right.

GRANDMA: Well, that's how it is when people call you up and ask you over to do something for them.

MRS BARKER: I suppose you're right, too. Well, Grandma, it's been very nice talking to you.

GRANDMA: And I've enjoyed listening. Say, don't tell Mommy or Daddy that I gave you that hint, will you?

MRS BARKER: Oh, dear me, the hint! I'd forgotten about it, if you can imagine such a thing. No, I won't breathe a word of it to them.

GRANDMA: I don't know if it helped you any . . .

MRS BARKER: I can't tell, yet. I'll have to . . . what *is* the word I want? . . . I'll have to relate it . . . that's it . . . I'll have to relate it to certain things that I *know*, and . . . draw . . . conclusions. . . . What I'll really have to do is to see if it applies to anything. I mean, after all, I *do* do volunteer work for an adoption service, but it isn't very much *like* the Bye-Bye Adoption Service . . . it *is* the Bye-Bye Adoption Service . . . and while I can remember Mommy and Daddy coming to see me, oh, about twenty years ago, about buying a bumble, I can't quite remember anyone very much *like* Mommy and Daddy coming to see me about buying a bumble. Don't you see? It really presents quite a problem. . . . I'll have to think about it . . . mull it . . . but at any rate, it was truly first-class of you to try to help me. Oh, will you still be here after I've had my drink of water?

GRANDMA: Probably . . . I'm not as spry as I used to be.

MRS BARKER: Oh. Well, I won't say good-bye then.

GRANDMA: No. Don't. [MRS BARKER *exits through the archway.*] People don't say good-bye to old people because they think they'll frighten them. Lordy! If they only knew how awful 'hello' and 'my, you're looking chipper' sounded, they wouldn't say those things either. The truth is, there isn't much you *can* say to old people that doesn't sound just terrible.

[*The doorbell rings.*]

Come on in!

[*The* YOUNG MAN *enters.* GRANDMA *looks him over.*]

Well, now, aren't you a breath of fresh air!

YOUNG MAN: Hello there.

GRANDMA: My, my, my. Are you the van man?

YOUNG MAN: The what?

GRANDMA: The van man. The van man. Are you come to take me away?

YOUNG MAN: I don't know what you're talking about.

GRANDMA: Oh. [*Pause.*] Well. [*Pause.*] My, my, aren't you something!

YOUNG MAN: Hm?

GRANDMA: I said, my, my, aren't you something.

YOUNG MAN: Oh. Thank you.

GRANDMA: You don't sound very enthusiastic.

YOUNG MAN: Oh, I'm . . . I'm used to it.

GRANDMA: Yup . . . yup. You know, if I were about a hundred and fifty years younger I could go for you.

YOUNG MAN: Yes, I imagine so.

GRANDMA: Unh-hunh . . . will you look at those muscles!

YOUNG MAN [*flexing his muscles*]: Yes, they're quite good, aren't they?

GRANDMA: Boy, they sure are. They natural?

YOUNG MAN: Well the basic structure was there, but I've done some work, too . . . you know, in a gym.

GRANDMA: I'll bet you have. You ought to be in the movies, boy.

YOUNG MAN: I know.

GRANDMA: Yup! Right up there on the old silver screen. But I suppose you've heard that before.

YOUNG MAN: Yes, I have.

GRANDMA: You ought to try out for them . . . the movies.

YOUNG MAN: Well, actually, I may have a career there yet. I've lived out on the West Coast almost all my life . . . and I've met a few people who . . . might be able to help me. I'm not in too much of a hurry, though. I'm almost as young as I look.

GRANDMA: Oh, that's nice. And will you look at that face!

YOUNG MAN: Yes, it's quite good, isn't it? Clean-cut, midwest farm boy type, almost insultingly good-looking in a typically American way. Good profile, straight nose, honest eyes, wonderful smile . . .

GRANDMA: Yup. Boy, you know what you are, don't you? You're the American Dream, that's what you are. All those other people, they don't know what they're talking about. You . . . *you* are the American Dream.

YOUNG MAN: Thanks.

MOMMY [*off stage*]: Who rang the doorbell?

GRANDMA [*shouting off stage*]: The American Dream!

MOMMY [*off stage*]: What? What was that, Grandma?

GRANDMA [*shouting*]: The American Dream! The American Dream! Damn it!

DADDY [*off stage*]: How's that, Mommy?

MOMMY [*off stage*]: Oh, some gibberish; pay no attention. Did you find Grandma's room?

DADDY [*off stage*]: No. I can't even find Mrs Barker.

YOUNG MAN: What was all that?

GRANDMA: Oh, that was just the folks, but let's not talk about them, honey; let's talk about you.

YOUNG MAN: All right.

GRANDMA: Well, let's see. If you're not the van man, what are you doing here?

YOUNG MAN: I'm looking for work.

GRANDMA: Are you! Well, what kind of work?

YOUNG MAN: Oh, almost anything . . . almost anything that pays. I'll do almost anything for money.

GRANDMA: Will you . . . will you? Hmmmm. I wonder if there's anything you could do around here?

YOUNG MAN: There might be. It looked to be a likely building.

GRANDMA: It's always looked to be a rather unlikely building to me, but I suppose you'd know better than I.

YOUNG MAN: I can sense these things.

GRANDMA: There *might* be something you could do around here. Stay there! Don't come any closer.

YOUNG MAN: Sorry.

GRANDMA: I don't mean I'd *mind*. I don't know whether I'd mind, or not. . . . But it wouldn't look well; it would look just *awful*.

YOUNG MAN: Yes; I suppose so.

GRANDMA: Now, stay there, let me concentrate. What could you do? The folks have been in something of a quandary around here today, sort of a dilemma, and I wonder if you mightn't be some help.

YOUNG MAN: I hope so . . . if there's money in it. Do you have any money?

GRANDMA: Money! Oh, there's more money around here than you'd know what to do with.

YOUNG MAN: I'm not so sure.

GRANDMA: Well, maybe not. Besides, I've got money of my own.

YOUNG MAN: You have?

GRANDMA: Sure. Old people quite often have lots of money; more often than most people expect. Come here, so I can whisper to you . . . not too close. I might faint.

YOUNG MAN: Oh, I'm sorry.

GRANDMA: It's all right, dear. Anyway . . . have you ever heard of that big baking contest they run? The one where all the ladies get together in a big barn and bake away?

YOUNG MAN: I'm . . . not . . . sure. . . .

GRANDMA: Not so close. Well, it doesn't matter whether you've heard of it or not. The important thing is – and I don't want anybody to hear this . . . the folks think I haven't been out of the house in eight years – the important thing is that I won first prize in that baking contest this year. Oh, it was in all the papers; not under my own name, though. I used a *nom de boulangère*; I called myself Uncle Henry.

YOUNG MAN: Did you?

GRANDMA: Why not? I didn't see any reason not to. I look just as much like an old man as I do like an old woman. And you know what I called it . . . what I won for?

YOUNG MAN: No. What did you call it?

GRANDMA: I called it Uncle Henry's Day-Old Cake.

YOUNG MAN: That's a very nice name.

GRANDMA: And it wasn't any trouble, either. All I did was go out and get a store-bought cake, and keep it around for a while, and then slip it in, unbeknownst to anybody. Simple.

YOUNG MAN: You're a very resourceful person.

GRANDMA: Pioneer stock.

YOUNG MAN: Is all this true? Do you want me to believe all this?

GRANDMA: Well, you can believe it or not . . . it doesn't make any difference to me. All *I* know is, Uncle Henry's Day-Old Cake won me twenty-five thousand smackerolas.

YOUNG MAN: Twenty-five thou–

GRANDMA: Right on the old loggerhead. Now . . . how do you like them apples?

YOUNG MAN: Love 'em.

GRANDMA: I thought you'd be impressed.

YOUNG MAN: Money talks.

GRANDMA: Hey! You look familiar.

YOUNG MAN: Hm? Pardon?

GRANDMA: I said, you look familiar.

YOUNG MAN: Well, I've done some modelling.

GRANDMA: No . . . no. I don't mean that. You look familiar.

YOUNG MAN: Well, I'm a type.

GRANDMA: Yup; you sure are. Why do you say you'd do anything for money . . . if you don't mind my being nosy?

YOUNG MAN: No, no. It's part of the interview. I'll be happy to tell you. It's that I have no talents at all, except what you see . . . my person; my body, my face. In every other way I am incomplete, and I must therefore . . . compensate.

GRANDMA: What do you mean, incomplete? You look pretty complete to me.

YOUNG MAN: I think I can explain it to you, partially because you're very old, and very old people have perceptions they keep to themselves, because if they expose them to other people . . . well, you know what ridicule and neglect are.

GRANDMA: I do, child, I do.

YOUNG MAN: Then listen. My mother died the night that I was born, and I never knew my father; I doubt my mother did. But, I wasn't alone, because lying with me . . . in the placenta . . . there was someone else . . . my brother . . . my twin.

GRANDMA: Oh, my child.

YOUNG MAN: We were identical twins . . . he and I . . . not fraternal . . . identical; we were derived from the same ovum; and in *this*, in that we were twins not from separate ova but from the same one, we had a kinship such as you cannot imagine. We . . . we felt each other breathe . . . his heartbeats thundered in my temples . . . mine in his . . . our stomachs ached and we cried for feeding at the same time . . . are you old enough to understand?

GRANDMA: I think so, child; I think I'm nearly old enough.

YOUNG MAN: I hope so. But we were separated when we were still very young, my brother, my twin and I . . . inasmuch as you can separate one being. We were torn apart . . . thrown to opposite ends of the continent. I don't know what became of my brother . . . to the rest of myself . . . except that, from time to time, in the years that have passed, I have suffered losses . . . that I can't explain. A fall from grace . . . a departure of innocence . . . loss . . . loss. How can I put it to you? All right; like this: Once . . . it was as if all at once my heart . . . became numb . . . almost as though I . . . almost as though . . . just like that . . . it had been wrenched from my body . . . and from that time I have been unable to love. Once . . . I was asleep at the time . . . I awoke, and my eyes were burning. And since that time I have been unable to see anything, *anything*, with pity, with affection . . . with anything but . . . cool disinterest. And my groin . . . even there . . . since one time . . . one specific agony . . . since then

I have not been able to *love* anyone with my body. And even my hands . . . I cannot touch another person and feel love. And there is more . . . there are more losses, but it all comes down to this: I no longer have the capacity to feel anything. I have no emotions. I have been drained, torn asunder . . . disembowelled. I have, now, only my person . . . my body, my face. I use what I have . . . I let people love me . . . I accept the syntax around me, for while I know I cannot relate . . . I know I must be related *to*. I let people love me . . . I let people touch me . . . I let them draw pleasure from my groin . . . from my presence . . . from the fact of me . . . but, that is all it comes to. As I told you, I am incomplete . . . I can feel nothing. I can feel nothing. And so . . . here I am . . . as you see me. I am . . . but this . . . what you see. And it will always be thus.

GRANDMA: Oh, my child; my child. [*Long pause; then*] I was mistaken . . . before. I don't know you from somewhere, but I knew . . . once . . . someone very much like you . . . or, very much as perhaps you were.

YOUNG MAN: Be careful; be very careful. What I have told you may not be true. In my profession . . .

GRANDMA: Shhhhhh. [*The* YOUNG MAN *bows his head, in acquiescence.*] Someone . . . to be more precise . . . who might have turned out to be very much like you might have turned out to be. And . . . unless I'm terribly mistaken . . . you've found yourself a job.

YOUNG MAN: What are my duties?

MRS BARKER [*off stage*]: Yoo-hoo! Yoo-hoo!

GRANDMA: Oh-oh. You'll . . . you'll have to play it by ear, my dear . . . unless I get a chance to talk to you again. I've got to go into my act, now.

YOUNG MAN: But, I . . .

GRANDMA: Yoo-hoo!

MRS BARKER [*coming through archway*]: Yoo-hoo . . . oh, there you are, Grandma. I'm glad to see somebody. I can't find Mommy or Daddy. [*Double takes.*] Well . . . who's this?

GRANDMA: This? Well . . . uh . . . oh, this is the . . . uh . . . the van man. That's who it is . . . the van man.

MRS BARKER: So! It's true! They *did* call the van man. They *are* having you carted away.

GRANDMA [*shrugging*]: Well, you know. It figures.

MRS BARKER [*to* YOUNG MAN]: How dare you cart this poor old woman away!

YOUNG MAN [*after a quick look at* GRANDMA, *who nods*]: I do what I'm paid to do. I don't ask any questions.

MRS BARKER [*after a brief pause*]: Oh. [*Pause.*] Well, you're quite right, of course, and I shouldn't meddle.

GRANDMA [*to* YOUNG MAN]: Dear, will you take my things out to the van? [*She points to the boxes.*]

YOUNG MAN [*after only the briefest hesitation*]: Why certainly.

GRANDMA [*as the* YOUNG MAN *takes up half the boxes, exits by the front door*]: Isn't that a nice young van man?

MRS BARKER [*shaking her head in disbelief, watching the* YOUNG MAN *exit*]: Unh-hunh . . . some things have changed for the better. I remember when I had *my* mother carted off . . . the van man who came for her wasn't anything near as nice as this one.

GRANDMA: Oh, did you have your mother carted off, too?

MRS BARKER [*cheerfully*]: Why certainly! Didn't you?

GRANDMA [*puzzling*]: No . . . no, I didn't. At least, I can't remember. Listen, dear; I got to talk to you for a second.

MRS BARKER: Why certainly, Grandma.

GRANDMA: Now, listen.

MRS BARKER: Yes, Grandma. Yes.

GRANDMA: Now listen carefully. You got this dilemma here with Mommy and Daddy . . .

MRS BARKER: Yes! I wonder where they've gone to.

GRANDMA: They'll be back in. Now, LISTEN!

MRS BARKER: Oh, I'm sorry.

GRANDMA: Now, you got this dilemma here with Mommy and Daddy, and I think I got the way out for you.

[*The* YOUNG MAN *re-enters through the front door.*]

Will you take the rest of my things out now, dear? [*To* MRS BARKER, *while the* YOUNG MAN *takes the rest of the boxes, exits again by the front door*] Fine. Now listen, dear. [*She begins to whisper in* MRS BARKER'S *ear.*]

MRS BARKER: Oh! Oh! Oh! I don't think I could . . . do you

really think I could? Well, why not? What a wonderful idea . . . what an absolutely wonderful idea!

GRANDMA: Well, yes, I thought it was.

MRS BARKER: And you so old!

GRANDMA: Heh, heh, heh.

MRS BARKER: Well, I think it's absolutely marvellous, anyway. I'm going to find Mommy and Daddy right now.

GRANDMA: Good. You do that.

MRS BARKER: Well, now. I think I will say good-bye. I can't thank you enough. [*She starts to exit through the archway.*]

GRANDMA: You're welcome. Say it!

MRS BARKER: Huh? What?

GRANDMA: Say good-bye.

MRS BARKER: Oh. Good-bye. [*She exits.*] Mommy! I say, Mommy! Daddy!

GRANDMA: Good-bye. [*By herself now, she looks about.*] Ah me. [*Shakes her head.*] Ah me. [*Takes in the room.*] Good-bye.
      [*The* YOUNG MAN *re-enters.*]

GRANDMA: Oh, hello, there.

YOUNG MAN: All the boxes are outside.

GRANDMA [*a little sadly*]: I don't know why I bother to take them with me. They don't have much in them . . . some old letters, a couple of regrets . . . Pekinese . . . blind at that . . . the television . . . my Sunday teeth . . . eighty-six years of living . . . some sounds . . . a few images, a little garbled by now . . . and, well . . . [*She shrugs.*] . . . you know . . . the things one accumulates.

YOUNG MAN: Can I get you . . . a cab, or something?

GRANDMA: Oh no, dear . . . thank you just the same. I'll take it from here.

YOUNG MAN: And what shall I do now?

GRANDMA: Oh, you stay here, dear. It will all become clear to you. It will be explained. You'll understand.

YOUNG MAN: Very well.

GRANDMA [*after one more look about*]: Well . . .

YOUNG MAN: Let me see you to the elevator.

GRANDMA: Oh . . . that *would* be nice, dear. [*They both exit by the front door, slowly.*]
      [*Enter* MRS BARKER, *followed by* MOMMY *and* DADDY.]

MRS BARKER: . . . and I'm happy to tell you that the whole thing's settled. Just like that.

MOMMY: Oh, we're so glad. We were afraid there might be a problem, what with delays, and all.

DADDY: Yes, we're very relieved.

MRS BARKER: Well, now; that's what professional women are for.

MOMMY: Why . . . where's Grandma? Grandma's not here! Where's Grandma? And look! The boxes are gone, too. Grandma's gone, and so are the boxes. She's taken off, and she's stolen something! Daddy!

MRS BARKER: Why, Mommy, the van man was here.

MOMMY [*startled*]: The what?

MRS BARKER: The van man. The van man was here.
[*The lights might dim a little, suddenly.*]

MOMMY [*shakes her head*]: No, that's impossible.

MRS BARKER: Why, I saw him with my own two eyes.

MOMMY [*near tears*]: No, no, that's impossible. No. There's no such thing as the van man. There is no van man. We . . . we made him up. Grandma? Grandma?

DADDY [*moving to* MOMMY): There, there, now.

MOMMY: Oh Daddy . . . where's Grandma?

DADDY: There, there, now.
[*While* DADDY *is comforting* MOMMY, GRANDMA *comes out, stage right, near the footlights.*]

GRANDMA [*to the audience*]: Shhhhhh! I want to watch this. [*She motions to* MRS BARKER *who, with a secret smile, tiptoes to the front door and opens it. The* YOUNG MAN *is framed therein. Lights up full again as he steps into the room.*]

MRS BARKER: Surprise! Surprise! Here we are!

MOMMY: What? What?

DADDY: Hm? What?

MOMMY [*her tears merely sniffles now*]: What surprise?

MRS BARKER: Why, I told you. The surprise I told you about.

DADDY: You . . . you know, Mommy.

MOMMY: Sur . . . prise?

DADDY [*urging her to cheerfulness*]: You remember, Mommy; why we asked . . . uh . . . what's-her-name to come here?

MRS BARKER: Mrs Barker, if you don't mind.

DADDY: Yes. Mommy? You remember now? About the bumble . . . about wanting satisfaction?

MOMMY [*her sorrow turning into delight*]: Yes. Why yes! Of course! Yes! Oh, how wonderful!

MRS BARKER [*to the* YOUNG MAN]: This is Mommy.

YOUNG MAN: How . . . how do you do?

MRS BARKER [*stage whisper*]: Her name's Mommy.

YOUNG MAN: How . . . how do you do, Mommy?

MOMMY: Well! Hello there!

MRS BARKER [*to the* YOUNG MAN]: And that is Daddy.

YOUNG MAN: How do you do, sir?

DADDY: How do you do?

MOMMY [*herself again, circling the* YOUNG MAN, *feeling his arm, poking him*]: Yes, sir! Yes, sirree! Now this is more like it. Now this is a great deal more like it! Daddy! Come see. Come see if this isn't a great deal more like it.

DADDY: I . . . I can see from here, Mommy. It does look a great deal more like it.

MOMMY: Yes, sir. Yes sirree! Mrs Barker, I don't know *how* to thank you.

MRS BARKER: Oh, don't worry about that. I'll send you a bill in the mail.

MOMMY: What this really calls for is a celebration. It calls for a drink.

MRS BARKER: Oh, what a nice idea.

MOMMY: There's some sauterne in the kitchen.

YOUNG MAN: I'll go.

MOMMY: Will you? Oh, how nice. The kitchen's through the archway there. [*As the* YOUNG MAN *exits: to* MRS BARKER] He's very nice. Really top notch; much better than the other one.

MRS BARKER: I'm glad you're pleased. And I'm glad everything's all straightened out.

MOMMY: Well, at least we know why we sent for you. We're glad that's cleared up. By the way, what's his name?

MRS BARKER: Ha! Call him whatever you like. He's yours. Call him what you called the other one.

MOMMY: Daddy? What did we call the other one?

DADDY [*puzzles*]: Why . . .

YOUNG MAN [*re-entering with a tray on which are a bottle of sauterne and five glasses*]: Here we are!

MOMMY: Hooray! Hooray!

MRS BARKER: Oh, good!

MOMMY [*moving to the tray*]: So, let's–. Five glasses? Why five? There are only four of us. Why five?

YOUNG MAN [*catches* GRANDMA'S *eye;* GRANDMA *indicates she is not there*]: Oh, I'm sorry.

MOMMY: You must learn to count. We're a wealthy family, and you must learn to count.

YOUNG MAN: I will.

MOMMY: Well, everybody take a glass. [*They do.*] And we'll drink to celebrate. To satisfaction! Who says you can't get satisfaction these days!

MRS BARKER: What dreadful sauterne!

MOMMY: Yes, isn't it? [*To* YOUNG MAN, *her voice already a little fuzzy from the wine*] You don't know how happy I am to see you! Yes sirree. Listen, that time we had with . . . with the other one. I'll tell you about it some time. [*Indicates* MRS BARKER] After she's gone. She was responsible for all the trouble in the first place. I'll tell you all about it. [*Sidles up to him a little.*] Maybe . . . maybe later tonight.

YOUNG MAN [*not moving away*]: Why yes. That would be very nice.

MOMMY [*puzzles*]: Something familiar about you . . . you know that? I can't quite place it. . . .

GRANDMA [*interrupting . . . to audience*]: Well, I guess that just about wraps it up. I mean, for better or worse, this is a comedy, and I don't think we'd better go any further. No, definitely not. So, let's leave things as they are right now . . . while everybody's happy . . . while everybody's got what he wants . . . or everybody's got what he thinks he wants. Good night, dears.

CURTAIN

JACK RICHARDSON

GALLOWS HUMOUR

A Play in Two Parts

For Harold Freeman

PREFACE

COMEDY is an illusive, arcane subject, lending itself to as many interpretations as there are senses of humour. Unlike tragedy, which resides behind the stern dicta of the academicians, subject only to the authority of Aristotle, comedy subjects itself to an empirical test every time it faces an audience. If smiles, chortles, or laughs are incited with some degree of intention by the doings on the stage, then, if we feel the need to push past enjoyment to criticism, we are up against the aesthetics of comedy. It may be comedy cautiously hyphenated or prefaced by the qualifiers 'tragi', 'high', 'low', 'sick', or 'drawing room', but it is comedy nevertheless. Such a capricious standard gives rise to a certain semantic laxity, and the playwright, after a perfunctory apology to the shades of Molière or Aristophanes, can apply the venerable name to his work without fear of being contradicted by anything save gloomy silence following what he considered his wittiest lines.

All this is by the way of easing *Gallows Humour* into a comic category. Writing it has amused me; reading it has caused a few of my friends to beg forgiveness for having thought me a taxing sobersides for so long a time. With such authority behind me, I might, with impunity, affix the words 'a comedy' after my title and rest secure in ambiguity until such time as the paying customer gives me the lie by a yawn or an anguished look at his watch.

All this would make judgement a simple process if there were not one important question left. Granting that a play passes the minimal standards set above, it is still to be evaluated in terms of good writing and bad; and here the waters grow a bit muddy, as no simple experiment, such as clocking the number of chuckles at five-minute intervals, will suffice. A baby can inspire laughter, but, maternal excesses aside, it is not a work of art. For such an evaluation, theory, the dark contradictory of humour, is, unfortunately, called for. Moreover, it is theory with precious little precedent or tradition to hide its flaws behind. Still, I imagine everyone who has tried to write lines that will amuse has one. I, for better or worse, have mine.

James Thurber, dealing gracefully with this knotty subject in a recent article, made a very useful suggestion to lexicographers and those who write about comedy. It was that 'tragi-comedy' should be written as one word, without the hyphen and all of a piece throughout. A simple suggestion but a provocative one; and by it I believe he means comedy is not something categorically separated from life's lamentations – something to be lowered into sub-plots for relief, a harmless, vapid antidote to the numbing effects of tragedy. Realist that he is, I believe Mr Thurber sees all too clearly how life entangles these two old dramatic opposites without regard to the well-made play or the Stagirite's compulsion for purity. To argue whether the natural balance favours one or the other is a barren enterprise: it is the temperament and selective vision of the artist that ultimately decides this question. However, if he can only discern one pattern for his art, then that art will be a limited one.

Now, if I may carry Mr Thurber's analysis a bit further, it also seems that comedy, on its highest level, has exactly the same kernel as its opposite – namely, the celebrated tragic flaw. The idealistic myopia of Don Quixote; the pathetic pretensions of Monsieur Jourdain; the chaotic hedonism of Falstaff – all of these are qualities which, had the eye viewing them not been a sly one, might have served tragic purposes; and the perceptive reader or listener will respond to the mixed origins of these works. On how this response is provoked, Shaw, as excellent a spectator of plays as he was a writer of them, spoke up for the art of comedy with the sentence, 'I go to the theatre to be moved to laughter, not to be tickled or bustled into it.'

The descent now from such theoretical peaks to the solid ground my play rests on covers a distance I would not care to measure. My critical side, for a moment freed from the simplicities of my plays, has abused its privilege. Any specific references to *Gallows Humour* with such absolutes as Cervantes, Molière, and Shakespeare still in the reader's mind would be an impertinence which no amount of Shavian bluster could make palatable. I've mentioned them not for the sake of any comparison, but to purge, if only for a moment, the term 'comedy' of all its Broadway connotations and to hint that, at its best level, the word is far more applicable to *Oedipus Rex* than to *Under the Yum-Yum Tree*. Simply watching a clown dash through the fundamentals of comedy should make this apparent. His slapstick inadequacies, as broadly stroked as they are, both touch and amuse; and the greater his talent, the more his inabilities to cope with whatever fates rule his particular world become a universal imitation of us all.

From clown to *Gallows Humour* makes a somewhat more logical transition than the previous paragraphs afforded, and I feel in this context certain comparisons could be made. I do not believe, however, that it is my function here to do so, and for those who would, I insist only that the very best and oldest clowns be chosen as examples. Clowns who, as I hope my play will, move the audience to laughter.

JACK RICHARDSON

First performed at the Gramercy Arts Theatre, New York, 18 April 1961.

CAST

PROLOGUE	*Paxton Whitehead*
LUCY	*Julie Bovasso*
WALTER	*Gerald Hiken*
WARDEN	*Vincent Gardenia*
MARTHA	*Julie Bovasso*
PHILLIP	*Gerald Hiken*

Directed by *George L. Sherman*

First performed in Britain at the Traverse Theatre Club, Edinburgh, August 1964.

Directed by *Charles Marowitz*

CHARACTERS

Part One

THE WARDEN
LUCY
WALTER

Part Two

THE WARDEN
PHILIP
MARTHA

PROLOGUE

An Actor, dressed in the costume of Death, steps before the curtain.

Ladies and gentlemen – a few words please. Now, those of you who are already beginning to fidget, squirm, and grumble about costume plays, let me begin by assuring you that I do not reappear this evening once the curtain has been raised. Indeed, it is only due to my sulking, fits of temper, and slight influence with the producer that I've managed to salvage this much of your attention from the play's remaining characters, whom all concerned found more entertaining, amusing, and dramatically effective than I. For, ladies and gentlemen, you see before you a part, a character, a creation, if you will, that has been cut – snipped out of the night's diversions by the author's second thoughts and placed here as an, we hope, inoffensive bonus, to be listened to or ignored at your pleasure. And *why* was this done, when you can see the expense I've gone to with my costume, the way I turn a phrase, and my rather relaxed manner in front of you which hints no little experience on the boards? Simply because I, I was considered too obvious, too blunt, too heavy-handed for a play struggling with your modern subtleties! My theatrical days, I was told, ended with the morality play, when other personae – Good Deeds, Knowledge, Earthly Pleasure, etc. – dragged their capitalized names and single dimensions across a bare stage, and I was well known about society as the great common denominator, familiar to everyone in the pit as that undernourished wag who skulked along the streets to the sound of flute and tabor, laying hands on kings and beggars, bishops and madmen, naughty nuns and clanking cavaliers. I was, you might say, a popular hero, and no one demanded any more from my appearances than that I stand as a reminder to the uncomfortable fact that life, with all its peculiar pleasures of the palace and the alehouse, has its dark and inevitable opposite. At times, I'll admit, the humour in these works was somewhat broad, and, on occasion, I was paired with an overbusty blonde *ingénue*, who, waving a few shocks of wheat in the air as a fertility symbol, would chase me about the stage to the low-bred delight of some rural audience. But such excesses were rare, and, more often, a healthy rapport was set up between the spectators and me which, while by no means making me immune from a few scattered jeers and catcalls, nevertheless allowed me to, as they say, get my laughs and make my point. But now, apparently, my point needs sharpening. Death is no longer something personal, something deeply etched, something old women claim they feel slipping lasciviously into their winter beds. Indeed, in the last years, I seem both to have expanded and blurred my activities without knowing it. The grave's dimensions suddenly have grown to include those who have not yet achieved the once necessary technicality of ceasing to breathe. It appears I now infiltrate those still bouncing to music, still kissing their wives, still wiggling their forefingers in the air to emphasize those final truths by which they think their lives are lived. But are they, after all, living? And if not, where does that leave me with my black-and-white attitude in the matter? It leaves me here, ladies and gentlemen, to deliver a poor prologue while the scenery is readied, while your tardy members stumble into their places, and the search begins for programmes that have already slipped beneath, behind, or between your seats. But I cannot really be too bitter. The anger of rejection having cooled, my healthy common sense tells me that I would have been truly out of place in a play designed for your tastes. For I confess that just yesterday, I – whom centuries have trained to recognize the precise moment when the eye's glaze, the hand's stiffness, and the mind's dimness announce another ghost has been given up to my charge – I made a total ass of myself by tugging away at a good dozen or so gentlemen who had no intention as yet of quitting this world. Looking at them, noticing all the old symptoms, I could have sworn they were ready, but that mistake was just one in a whole series ranging from hospitals to beauty salons that I've been making recently with my old-fashioned methods. That one-time basic distinction between the quick and the dead has become far too abstract today for one with my earthbound mind, and this fundamental confusion was, I fear, showing up in my performances. For even on the stage, in a play darkened by the shadow of a gallows, I, so perfectly at home in such a setting, now find it difficult, with my ancient eyes, to tell the hangman from the hanged. I hope, for my future and peace of mind, that you, the author's contemporaries, do not.

[*Death exits, drawing the curtain as he does so.*]

PART ONE

The lights come up upon a prison cell. There is a small washbasin to the right, and, standing close against the centre wall, there is a razor-thin cot. Above the monkish bed is the room's sole window, barred into sections, through which one can see that it is night outside. At the room's left is the cell door, and behind it the beginning of an outside corridor. In this passageway, looking into the cell, stand a man and woman. Next to them, on a little portable tray, is a large platter decked with silver Queen Anne cover dishes, sauceboats, etc. The man, comfortably stout, seems expansively contented with himself. He is smiling broadly. The woman, attired in a bright yellow blouse and tight black skirt, has a thin face of angle and bone which is well covered with cosmetics. Her age is indeterminate, and she is beautiful in the way a carnival mask is so.

They are looking at WALTER, *who is sitting on the cell's cot. He has the jacket of his prison suit in his lap and is attending to it with needle and thread. Caught in his undershirt, he seems very pale and fragile. His face is unremarkably inoffensive, and covered with the scribbling of a fifty-year-old life. As he sews, he hums to himself.*

> [*After several seconds, the man, the* WARDEN, *and the woman,* LUCY, *begin to speak.*]

WARDEN: There he is, Lucy. Let's hope this one doesn't prove too difficult for you.

LUCY: Now what could someone who looks like that do to be hanged?

WARDEN [*chuckling*]: He beat his wife to death with a golf club – forty-one strokes from the temple to the chin.

> [*At this point* WALTER'S *humming rises a bit in pitch and volume.*]

LUCY: What a nice smile he has, and how thin his arms are. They're not tattooed either.

WARDEN [*smiling, but a bit impatient*]: Now, Lucy, it's romantic notions like that that get you into trouble. If you start thinking of murderers as upper-middle-class types you'll be more successful at your work.

LUCY [*indignant*]: I haven't done too bad up till now. There aren't many women, even in the trade, that can take a man's mind off your gallows when he's got less than two hours to go.

WARDEN [*in an apologetic tone*]: Oh, you're a professional, all right; they just don't cut them like you any more. But sometimes I wonder if you weren't better suited to those naughty houses stuffed with incense, beaded curtains, and overhead mirrors. Maybe you're just not up to making love surrounded by four grey walls.

LUCY: Listen, Warden, I've had my victories in here too.

WARDEN: Yes, but the state's gone to a great deal of trouble bringing you ladies up here to serve as little humanizing morsels for those it's going to hang. Your whole purpose is to make these poor fellows' last hours so heady, so full of pleasure that they just float up those stairs and smile into the dull, commonplace face of our hangman. Making love to you, Lucy, is supposed to accomplish this. And yet the last two you handed over to us behaved abominably: they shuffled by those sentimental journalists looking as if they were already dead. You know what the press can do with that; and then all our good intentions are forgotten.

LUCY: I couldn't get near those two. They just weren't interested.

WARDEN [*in a slightly threatening tone*]: It's your job to make them interested, Lucy.

LUCY: Now what could I do? One was over seventy, after all, and the other told me he hadn't made love to anything since he saw his cat's hysterectomy scars.

WARDEN: You were picked for this official work because you seemed to have experience with difficult types. Remember where you were when we found you? Standing in a doorway with a scraggly piece of fur around your neck and runs in your stockings. Even in the city's poorest section you weren't turning customers away, were you? And if you had to go back to it . . .

LUCY: All right, Warden, you've made your point.

WARDEN: Just a little warning, Lucy. You know how I'd hate to fire you.

LUCY: All right, all right. Now, is there anything I should know about our man in there?

WARDEN: Oh, you should really find him easy to deal with. He's been most co-operative since being with us: never cried when appeals were turned down, never spat his food back at the guards, never used the walls for thumb-nosing little phrases at the world – no, he's been a perfect sort up till now.

LUCY: Good, I don't like those who have an axe to grind. They never stop talking long enough for anything to really get going between us.

WARDEN: Well, Walter there's one of the better sort, all right, that's why you were assigned to him. You used to do so well with educated types. I remembered that physicist you went after a few years ago – for six months he moped about his cell, mumbling to himself. But after you were through with him he died happily explaining the theory of sub-atomic particles to our executioner. You'd turned a homicidal maniac back into a useful man.

LUCY: I just got his mind back on fundamentals. That seems to pep his type up.

WARDEN: Well, that's what I want you to do for Walter. [*Tapping one of the cover dishes*] I had our chef up all night working on the fried chicken in here, but I hope he'll enjoy you even more. I sort of like this one and want him to have a little fling before he's hanged.

LUCY [*flatly*]: Oh, you have a big heart under that forty-dollar suit, Warden.

WARDEN: Why, thank you, Lucy. Sometimes I think it goes unnoticed.

LUCY: Now, shall I get to work?

WARDEN: All right, we might as well start the introductions. Ah, would you wheel his dinner in to him? I think the silver trays will set you off to advantage. [*The* WARDEN *extracts a key, opens the cell door, and he and* LUCY *enter.* WALTER, *his sewing in his hands, jumps up abruptly to meet them. He then follows* LUCY *with his eyes as, smiling, she wheels the tray past him into the lower left corner of the cell.*] Hello, Walter, how's it going today?

WALTER [*still trying to keep an eye on* LUCY *who, after leaving the tray, begins walking about the cell, tapping at the walls and poking at the cot*]: Warden, nice of you to come by. Is it time already?

WARDEN: Heavens, no; you still have nearly two hours. Some insects, I'm told, live an entire life through in less time – birth, copulation, and death, all counted off in seconds.

WALTER [*pleasantly, but still with an eye on* LUCY *who is beginning to prop up the pillow on his cot*]: That sounds like a very nice arrangement.

WARDEN: Right! After all, who needs years but those who have to repeat themselves?

LUCY [*stepping back from the cot and examining it*]: You're talking on my time, Warden.

WARDEN: Quite so, Lucy, quite so. Walter, I'd like you to meet Lucy. She's going to stay here with you until the end – compliments of the state.

WALTER: With me? But I don't understand.

WARDEN: No effusions of gratitude, Walter. No man should eat his last meal without a little female company.

WALTER: Do you mean she's to – to . . .?

WARDEN [*nodding*]: It's an innovation in our penal programme. Takes some of the sting out of anti-capital punishment arguments. Sending a man out to die with a Lucy still fresh in every part of him – well, nothing cold-blooded about that, is there? Everything else about the little ceremony is, I'll admit, rather cut and dried, a bit too much so, even for my taste. That's what puts people off about it. The clack of the guard's shoes in cadence over those cobblestones, the same number of steps to be climbed, the ritual last trite phrases – no, there's not much spice in it any more. But with this new little prologue we've added – well, it seems to keep the others like you, Walter, from being swallowed up in formality. There's something touchingly human about the whole affair when Lucy and her kind deliver you back to our official hands.

LUCY [*walking back to the tray of food, she opens a cover dish*]: And it keeps girls like me off the street. Hmm! This will get cold if you don't start on it, Walter.

WALTER: Oh, I'm not really hungry.

WARDEN: But that's fried chicken in there. With a heavy crust.

WALTER: I know I ordered it, but you won't mind if I just don't begin right away.

LUCY: Well, you've no complaints if I have a leg then, do you? Being up this early in the morning always gives me an [*She says the word with a seductive smile at* WALTER.] appetite.

WALTER: No, no; go right ahead.

WARDEN [*watching* LUCY *as she takes a large bite*]: Look at her go after that chicken, Walter. How many men would love to be in that piece of meat's place. And you're going to get the chance.

WALTER: Well, that's very nice, and I'm grateful to both of you; but I really don't . . .

WARDEN: Come now, Walter, no protests. Lucy there brings a little unpremeditated dash into the dull cubes and well-scrubbed-down corridors of our prison. You've been here so long I'll bet you've forgotten what a woman like Lucy, wrapped snugly in a yellow blouse and black skirt, can mean.

WALTER [*backing away and waving his hand in protest*]: Oh, no, I haven't.

LUCY [*taking a few tentative dance steps*]: Do you know, it's a pity you can't have music piped in here. It would be nice to dance a bit before settling down to work, wouldn't it, Walter?

WALTER: I can't dance, really.

WARDEN: Well, then, she could teach you. After all, there's always time to learn something new. But now, now that a festive note's been struck in the cell, I guess I'm what they call *de trop*. Well, now, enjoy each other. [*Pointing a preceptorial finger at* WALTER] I want to see a contented face, Walter, when I return.

WALTER: Doesn't it seem contented now?

WARDEN [*studying* WALTER'S *face*]: It seems a little pinched and furrowed to me. Not the way one looks when Lucy's through with him.

WALTER: I can smile a bit if you want.

WARDEN: Save all that for the lady there. [*Stepping back and looking at the two of them*] Ah, actually you make a fine-looking couple together. You know, it's moments like this that make a welfare state seem worth while after all. [*The* WARDEN *leaves.*]

LUCY [*throwing the chicken bone over her shoulder onto the floor*]: God! I'd starve if he had to pimp for me.

WALTER [*quickly going over and retrieving the bone and putting it back on the tray*]: Please, I'm trying to leave a tidy cell behind me.

LUCY: Well, sorry!

WALTER: I don't mean to be rude, but you'd be surprised how hard it is keeping a little place like this in order.

LUCY [*a little confused*]: You give it a scrubbing once a day?

WALTER: Yes, but that won't do it. Every time a guard comes in here, some of the lint from his uniform stays behind. [*Tracing the descent of an imaginary piece of lint with his finger*] You can see it floating down from a sleeve or a lapel, but once it hits the grey floor it's the devil to find.

LUCY [*looking down at where* WALTER'S *finger last traced the lint*]: I can see it could be a problem.

WALTER: But please don't let me stop you from finishing the chicken if you want to. Just be careful the crust doesn't splatter.

LUCY: But that's *your* last meal, after all, Walter.

WALTER: Oh, I'm afraid I ordered that in a fit of absence of mind. Fried foods raise the deuce with my stomach.

LUCY: Begins to ache?

WALTER: No, just snarl. It lasts for days, and, in company, believe me, it can be very embarrassing.

LUCY [*after a pause in which she watches* WALTER *continue his sewing*]: Well, then, if no food, how about a cigarette before we begin?

WALTER: No, thank you. And if you're going to, be careful of the ashes. There's a little can underneath the sink you can use.

LUCY [*returning the cigarettes to her dress pocket, she turns away from* WALTER]: Jesus! [*Hunching her shoulders, she shivers and takes a few halting dance steps*] You've got to keep moving to stay warm in here.

WALTER: That blouse you're wearing must be very thin.

LUCY [*brightening*]: Well, finally noticing that there's a woman in here with you?

WALTER [*dropping his eyes back to the sewing*]: Tell me, do you really do this sort of work often for the prison?

LUCY: I've signed a five-year contract. And, as I'm not getting any younger, it's turned out to be a pretty good arrangement. In the last year, though, I've been kept a little too busy. It must have been the moon phases or something, but it seems as if everybody was cementing mothers up in the basement, shooting politicians, or setting fire to their friends. I hope things begin to calm down a bit now.

WALTER: But isn't it dangerous to come into a confined place with men who are going to be hanged in a matter of hours?

LUCY [*as she sits next to* WALTER *on the cot*]: No more dangerous than the streets in the summer season. I'll take a cell with a man in it who's butchered an even dozen five-year-olds to a boulevard stuffed with tourists waving credit cards in one hand and pinching with the other. No, by the time a man reaches this cell, Walter, the violence he had in him has wasted away. It's been used up on his victim, the judge, his childhood, his shoes, and God knows what else. There's nothing but the lamb left when I arrive.

WALTER: The lamb?

LUCY: I don't mean that in a bad sense now. It's just that, for a woman who doesn't like to be treated roughly, I find men who use this cell have very gentle hands.

WALTER [*looking at his hands*]: Mine are a bit rough from all the floor scrubbing I've done. Prison soap isn't the best.

LUCY [*taking his hands*]: They look as soft as cats' paws to me.

WALTER [*pulling his hands away, he inches back from* LUCY *and takes a big stitch in his sewing*]: You must excuse me, but I have to finish this little job of mending.

LUCY: I never thought I'd have to compete with a needle and thread, Walter.

WALTER: My number-patch was loose. I was afraid it might fall off during the – well, ceremonies.

LUCY: Your number-patch?

WALTER [*defensively*]: It's very important that this number stays on me. This is how I'm identified in I don't know how many files and on dozens of official cards. 43556 is the key to my ending life on the proper line in the ledger, and I've grown quite fond of it.

LUCY [*humouring Walter*]: 43556 – it has a nice ring to it. Better than a number packed with a lot of zeros.

WALTER: Well, actually, I would have preferred one with all even numbers, but it would have seemed fussy, I suppose, to insist on it.

LUCY [*moving closer to* WALTER *and beginning to stroke his neck*]: Well, now, why don't you put your sewing away and let me show you why the prison officials chose me out of over a thousand applicants for my job.

WALTER [*jumping up from the cot*]: Oh, no, Lucy, that's quite out of the question.

LUCY [*just a slight touch of impatience showing*]: Now listen, Walter . . .

WALTER: Oh, it's certainly nothing personal. [*Staring firmly at Lucy*] You do make that blouse and skirt seem wrapped around perfect treasures, and your skin is beautifully pale and, I'm sure, exciting to stroke for hours, even with my rather insensitive hands. [*Pulling himself together*] But, no, I just don't wish to.

LUCY [*smoothing out her blouse*]: Well, from the description, there isn't any doubt that you at least like women.

WALTER: Oh I do; or, rather, I did. But that's all over now.

LUCY [*getting up and moving towards* WALTER]: But it doesn't have to be over. There's still a little time left. You probably have a miniature gallows dancing in front of your eyes, and you think it's numbed those important little nerves for good. But, believe me, Lucy can start them twitching again. I've done it for dozens of others far more upset about dying than you seem to be.

WALTER [*backing away from her*]: But I don't want them to start twitching now.

LUCY: After they begin, then you'll want, Walter.

WALTER: No, no; I just want to remain peaceful.

LUCY: Peaceful? How can you use that word, when, in not too much more than an hour, you'll drag yourself up those thirteen steps?

WALTER [*backed against the cell's left wall, he clutches his jacket, thread and needle in front of him*]: You couldn't understand, Lucy. Being peaceful would just bore you.

LUCY: Nothing bores me, Walter. That's why I'm a success in my business.

WALTER: Please! Stay back a bit. I can hear you breathing.

LUCY: It's a nice sound, isn't it? My lungs, in fact all the machinery inside me, Walter, work perfectly.

WALTER: I'm sure; but I don't want to listen to their sounds. One of the advantages of a cell is its quiet. I've grown used to silence.

LUCY [*rubbing his arm and speaking in a coaxing voice*]: But my reputation's at stake, Walter. One failure leaves a permanent mark on one in my profession. I'd have to take to deeper layers of rouge, longer eyelashes, and darker stockings. My fur coat would need more padding at the shoulders and the heels on my shoes would be raised an inch at the very least. You wouldn't want to cause that, would you, Walter? You wouldn't want to start Lucy off looking for wigs and stronger perfumes?

WALTER [*pleading*]: The scent you're wearing is making me dizzy enough as it is.

LUCY: There, you see, those nerves aren't dead. They're coming back to us after all.

WALTER [*trying, but not succeeding, to remove her hand*]: Please, I'm just 43556; you can't expect a number to make love.

LUCY [*tripping her finger across his chest*]: I'm not touching a number now, am I? No, this is the body of a man. A little out of condition, maybe, from being closed up in a cell for months, but it still reacts to my fingers, doesn't it?

WALTER [*as though suffering, he looks down at* LUCY'S *bosom*]:
Oh, I've always been partial to women of your build, with
your hair; and underneath that powder, I can see freckles.
For me, freckles were always an irresistible aphrodisiac.

LUCY: Well, those freckles, my fingers, everything's yours,
Walter. Just forget where you are, and think of trombones,
bourbon bottles, and street-cars crowded with wet people
starting off on a Saturday night.

WALTER [*rigid, with his eyes closed*]: People forgetting who,
what, or where they've been. All getting into new skins,
expressions, and troubles. But wanting to laugh through it
all.

LUCY: That's it, Walter. Laughing when you slip on the
dance floor, find your socks don't match or that you can't
make love more than twice a night.

WALTER [*now happily, but painfully, reminiscing*]: And the Chinese
restaurants you mistake for your house and the hands, often
with gloves on them, you grab hold of.

LUCY [*whispering in* WALTER'S *ear*]: And now stop talking,
Walter, and let's . . .

WALTER [*sticking her in the back with his needle*]: No! Get away
from me. [*He breaks loose and moves to the centre of the cell.*]

LUCY [*with a loud yell*]: Why, you crazy–. That was a sharp
needle you stuck in me!

WALTER [*keeping the needle poised for attack*]: And I'll do it again
if you come after me. This is my cell – ten paces wide,
twenty long. Nothing, absolutely nothing unexpected
happens here.

LUCY [*feeling the wounded spot on her back*]: God, I think I'm
bleeding.

WALTER: Oh, no; no blood, please. I've seen all the blood I
ever want to see.

LUCY: Then you shouldn't go about sticking people with
needles or hitting them with golf clubs.

WALTER: You know about that?

LUCY [*somewhat abstracted as she rubs her wound and examines her
hand*]: It's written right across your forehead. [*Examining
and rubbing her fingers together*] Well, I'm not bleeding after
all.

WALTER: I'm grateful for that at least. I'm afraid I just lost my head for a moment. I felt myself slipping back into everything this cell protects me from, and I. . . . Are you angry with me, Lucy?

LUCY [*dismissing the incident*]: Oh, I've had worse done to me by clients with sort of Victorian tastes in love. But you *have* disappointed me, Walter. I thought we'd strike it off right away.

WALTER: Oh, you wouldn't have found me much good any-way. My wife used to make me take pills . . .

LUCY: For God's sake, no talk about the wife, especially one whose skull you split open. It's professionally insulting after being stuck with your needle.

WALTER: Well, I just thought to pass the time . . .

LUCY: Clients talk about their wives *after* making love. [*As if pondering a new discovery*] Wives and post-coital depression seem to go together. [*Now back to lecturing* WALTER *on his brothel manners*] But before, it's themselves they take apart and it's our job to put them back together again.

WALTER: Well, all my pieces are in their proper place and I don't want them disarranged.

LUCY [*sweetly*]: No one wants to do that, Walter. Perhaps I did rush you a little bit; but, after all, you're the one counting the minutes and I thought you'd want them stuffed with all the things your clean little cell's been lacking.

WALTER: I'd already planned how to use every second of them before you arrived: there was the number-patch to be sewn on, shoes to be polished, a final stroll four times around the cell, and then I was going to wash, which, because of the soap's poor quality, would most likely have taken me up to the time the warden and his guards came for me.

LUCY: Well, it *is* asking a lot wanting you to give up all those wild plans for me.

WALTER [*nodding in agreement*]: I'll already have to pass up the shoes.

LUCY: Well, give up two of your laps around the room and talk a little about yourself. At least let me show you how well I've been trained as a sympathetic listener.

WALTER: Why, there's nothing much to say about me.

LUCY [*coaxingly*]: Oh, come on; start off with the kind of job you used to have.

WALTER: Well, I was a moderately successful lawyer.

LUCY [*laughing*]: A lawyer?

WALTER [*a little anxiously*]: Why are you laughing?

LUCY: Well, being here – that doesn't say much for your ability to sway juries, does it?

WALTER [*testily*]: I didn't defend myself; and, besides, I was irrefutably guilty.

LUCY: I thought it was always easier to win defending a guilty man than an innocent one.

WALTER [*slightly outraged at this*]: Now, you see, it's just that sort of over-the-shoulder attitude that's turned our laws into a fool's game today.

LUCY: You mean like the city ordinance against soliciting on the streets? I've always thought that one was woolly-headed.

WALTER [*wagging his head impatiently*]: I'm not talking about your particular likes and dislikes, Lucy. It's the nature of the law that's been abused.

LUCY: The jails seem full enough to me.

WALTER [*growing a little more excited*]: No, no; laws are supposed to be as solid and immovable as these walls. At least that's what I thought when I began studying them. They weren't supposed to depend upon the judge's sinus condition, a lady juror's two Caesareans, or poor air conditioning in the courtroom. They were to be hermetically sealed – untouched by human hands.

LUCY: Calm down a bit, Walter.

WALTER [*now waving his arms*]: But don't you see they weren't? They were worthless little hide-and-seek rules made up to give the neighbourhood's poor children something to do in the evenings. No god had bellowed them out or burned them into a mountain.

LUCY: Be careful you don't stick yourself with the needle.

WALTER [*now quite intense*]: Oh, listen to me, Lucy. Can you understand what it meant to a man devoted to the law to find out it was all one big caprice? It was as if you looked up suddenly at a night sky and saw every planet and star dancing drunkenly about.

LUCY [*smiling invitingly*]: That might be exciting, Walter. And sometimes, making love out of doors, when the weather permitted, I think I did see the stars wiggle a bit.

WALTER [*angry at* LUCY's *non sequitur*]: Wiggle, do they? Well, that's not going to happen here! Not in this cell. [*He jumps up on the cot and points to the barred window*] Look through this window, Lucy. See how the sky's sectioned into nine perfect squares? On a clear night each square contains exactly five stars and the centre one has a planet all to itself.

LUCY: A planet? Which one?

WALTER: A sexless one; far from the sun, always cold, but giving off a dull, dependable light. [*Patting the bars*] No, these little bars are particular about what they let into their boundaries.

LUCY [*temporarily defeated*]: All right, let's skip love for a while.

WALTER [*somewhat calmer, he comes down from the cot*]: The law had most of my love. I believed all one had to do was match little scraps of fact against those fine, heavily punctuated sentences in the books and, like a candy machine, the right answer would come out neatly wrapped. Oh, you don't know how snugly I fitted into everything then. With those laws standing firm, all their lesser relatives, from chemistry formulas to table manners, seemed impregnable. In those days I knew exactly what to pray for, how often a month I should have sex (four times, only with my wife), and how stern I should be when my children spilled their soup. I knew who was the villain and who the virgin on the stage; I knew my laundry would come back on time without a piece missing; and I knew that every mirror would reflect at me a recognizable, satisfied face that had aged just the right amount since last being seen. Oh, Lucy, everything from constellation to subways seemed to be moving at my rhythm. And then . . . then . . .

LUCY: And then?

WALTER [*bitterly*]: And then came the Gogarty trial.

LUCY: A trial for murder?

WALTER [*beginning wistfully, then gradually growing more involved*]: No, a suit for damages. Mrs Ellen Gogarty versus The Municipal Bus Company – that was its official title. The woman's son, age thirty-five, had been run over and completely mashed by one of their vehicles. The light had been with him, and the bus driver, by eyewitness account, had been drunk and singing 'Little Alice Bottom' when the accident took place. I was whistling the same tune when, these bits of evidence snapped inside my brief case, I arrived at the courthouse on a morning that seemed no different from a thousand others. I even remember exchanging a joke with one of the guards and making a date with the opposing attorney, who was putting up only a token defence, for dinner that evening. Then the trial began: the judge smiled at me, the jury nodded in solemn agreement as I turned phrases and probed witnesses. With every second our case was strengthened, and, throughout the examinations, Mrs Gogarty, wearing a new but inexpensive summer hat and asking only to be recompensed for the loss of her only son, sat soaking up sympathetic stares from everyone in the court. The case, as they say, was open and shut. Open and shut.

LUCY [*who has been sitting on the cot, listening intently*]: And what happened?

WALTER [*now incensed over the memory*]: Hiccups! Hiccups! Just before the jury was about to file out, Mrs Gogarty began to hiccup. Oh, at first, it was hardly noticeable; but then they became louder and more frequent. I waved a warning finger at her to be silent, but she blinked back that she couldn't help herself; and while the jury stood stunned in their places, the gulping sounds went on jerking her frail little body this way and that. Finally, they actually came to be syncopated – two short, one long; one long, three short; two long. [*He puts his hands to his ears.*] And with the occasional change in pitch there was almost a little tune coming out of her. Sometimes I can still hear it, sounding like a street calliope; and then comes the laughter: first from the spectators in the court, then from the members of the jury, and, finally, from the judge himself. I try to speak, to read a few apposite remarks on courtroom behaviour from the law book on my desk, but I'm literally drowned out with laughter. And through it all, like some devilish timpani in an orchestra, Mrs Gogarty's hiccups, keeping up their erratic beat and brutal melody–. [*He raises and drops his voice so the outline of a tune can be heard.*] One long, one short; two long, one short. . . . [*Here he pauses and collects himself.*] Snorting, slapping each other's back and nudging one another's ribs, the jury files out of the room. The wait is a very short one, and from behind the jury-chamber door come the sounds of still more snickers with an occasional imitation of my client's disorder. Finally, as if they'd been off on a party – collars open, ties askew, hair undone – the men and women who are to decide our case return and, while Mrs Gogarty goes on with those loud little spasms, they announce a verdict against her. I can't believe it and, throwing protocol to the winds, ask why. 'How can she be suffering grief worth any compensation at all when she hiccups?' so says the jury foreman. 'Madness,' I answer and turn to the judge. 'My good sir,' he says, chuckling like an idiot, 'she really did hiccup out a little tune.' 'The law!' I cry. 'Hiccups!' he answers, and the laughter starts all around again. [*Slowly now, as if looking in the narration of simple fact for a solution*] I went to the governor himself, Lucy. I showed him there was nothing in the pertinent judicial paragraphs about this involuntary closure of the glottis and the noise produced therefrom, and *he* answered that those paragraphs were to be amended to include the peculiar Gogarty phenomenon. I knew then that it was all over, and that a sneeze, hiccup, or crooked nose could twist those impressive sentences into gibberish.

[*There is silence for a moment, and then* LUCY *rises from the cot and makes an attempt at consolation.*]

LUCY: Maybe it's better that way. After all, that's what makes a day interesting. It's the little unexpected matters of taste, like a man going wild over a mole on your chin, that keeps the beauty contest also-rans like me in business.

WALTER [*sadly*]: I knew you'd think that, Lucy; but, for me, Mrs Gogarty's hiccups were the end of everything. I no longer knew what clubs to join, what tie to choose, what toothpaste to use, what church to go to. At home, where I always thought things went smoothly and orderly, I suddenly found my children snipping off our dog's tail an inch a day with a pair of scissors, writing obscene couplets on my shirt collars, biting my leg whenever I passed by, and singing marching songs from the War of 1812. And my wife's birthmark, a little red triangle that had always been tucked inconspicuously behind her left ear, began turning up in the centre of her forehead, in the middle of her stomach, and on the soles of her feet . . .

LUCY [*now a little impatient with him*]: Are we going back to the wife again?

WALTER [*growing excited again*]: My life was formless, a tiny piece of chaos. What was left to me that couldn't be hiccuped out of existence? Right and left, buy and sell, love and hate – these now meant nothing to me. I found myself on the wrong trains, in the wrong beds, with the wrong people. And my neighbourhood, my neighbourhood that I had helped zone to perfection, became a carnival of the lowest sort, and my neighbours, whom I knew inside and out, danced about beneath layer on layer of holiday masks until I couldn't tell one from the other. And then, God knows when or where it happened, I found a mirror sending back at me a face that I had never seen before – a face with wild eyes, bristling hair, and a heavy growth of stubble – a face I would have crossed the street to avoid had I seen it coming at me in happier times. Oh, I'd been cheated, Lucy, and gradually I began to grow angry – mad, in fact – until one morning, with everything spinning about me in complete disorder, I struck back. My poor wife happened to be closest at hand, and for all I know I might have thought I was on the golf course until I felt the club make contact with her skull. I remember it sounding as if it were a good shot, and then I looked up to follow the ball's flight and found . . .

LUCY: That's enough, Walter! I'm beginning to shiver.

WALTER [*recalled from his memories*]: But now comes the pleasant part.

LUCY [*shaking her head as if to clear it*]: No, for me, the goodies in your story are over.

WALTER: No, no; don't you see? The law came back to me. Everything began falling in line again. I have my number, a room that never changes, meals that arrive punctually to the moment, and guards whose manners are perfectly predictable. [*With weak joy*] The world has boundaries again and I know my place in it.

LUCY [*almost threateningly*]: In one hour your place will be at the end of a rope.

WALTER [*with military stiffness*]: But my death will take place according to a rigid schedule and then be *officially* recorded. What more could I want?

LUCY [*with desperate hope*]: A little sex?

WALTER [*vexed at this*]: Good God! have you understood nothing? That belongs to the dizziness on the other side of those walls. Here, in my prison, the laws hold, and I won't have them disturbed by perfume and overpowdered flesh.

LUCY [*now angry*]: Oh, won't you? Do you know, if they came in this minute with a rope ready, it'd be my overpowdered flesh they'd hang? Yes, they'd be looking for something live to string up, Walter, and you certainly don't pass the test.

WALTER: I know what being alive means to you.

LUCY [*beginning to unwrap the belt from around her waist*]: Oh, between Mrs Gogarty's lost case and your wife's murder you had a taste of it, all right; but it frightened you right into this cell.

WALTER [*showing apprehension*]: What on earth are you doing? You're not going to undress? I promise you it won't do any good.

LUCY: I'm not understanding you, Walter. And, as a client, you have a right to that from me. I'm going to try to shorten the distance between us. [*She steps upon the cot, loops one end of the belt, and fastens the other to one of the bars across the window.*]

WALTER: You'll leave footprints on the pillow!

LUCY: You won't be using it again, Walter. I just want to see how it'd feel with a noose around my neck. Who knows? Maybe you're right; maybe the only thing I'd worry about is that they got my name and number right on the morgue card. [*She slips the belt over her head.*] There, it's in place; the hangman's taken his hands from my shoulders, the sack's dropped over my eyes; my shoes, just polished, are shining in the morning light . . .

WALTER: Stop it! Stop it! You're just pretending anyway.

LUCY [*in the tones of a spoiled little girl*]: I'm in a cell with a murderer. How do I know you won't push the cot out from under me?

WALTER: I might do just that.

LUCY [*with her eyes shut and her head tilted back*]: I will drop down, happy that the sky I leave behind has nice equal sections, each with so many numbers of stars. I'll be content that my dying has an alphabetical standing, that my last meal came to me on time, that my cell is immaculate, that the prison day which I'll never see will be like all the others I've lived through, and that I didn't sweat, sing, throw up, or make love to a woman. So then, let the trap doors fly open underneath me. With no regrets about this life, I'll die happily. [*Pause.*] The hell I will!

WALTER [*walking up to cot and threatening to kick one of its legs*]: If you don't come down, I swear I'll kick the cot out from under you, Lucy.

LUCY [*removing the belt from around her neck*]: You bet I'll come down. Dying with your point of view really makes me sick to my stomach. [*She steps down and walks as far away from* WALTER *as the confines of the cell permit.*]

WALTER [*somewhat meek and apologetic*]: I'm not trying to convert you to anything, after all.

LUCY: No, you're not. You're too happy curled up in your little womb to want company.

WALTER: Please, no coarse talk, Lucy.

LUCY: Oh, of course not. You'd like to have a conversation in algebra equations, I'll bet. Well, I'm not going to let you get away with it.

WALTER [*puzzled and on the defensive*]: Why are you attacking me?

LUCY: Because you remind me of a *happy* 'still-life' whore, Walter. Do you know what that is? It's the last step for all of us in this business. When even the streets won't have you and you've lost your nerve for the river, then it's a twenty-four-hour-in-bed house for you. You don't own anything to wear except a grease-stained kimono the madam gives you; there's no make-up on the little table next to you, no mirror, the room's always dark, and the only sounds are the footsteps in the corridor that shuffle, with sometimes just a little hesitation, past your door that's been locked from the outside. You just lie there, Walter, waiting for the lock to click open, letting another client in at you. Oh, and there's no worry about these men like there is when you're on your own. You don't fret over whether or not he's a handsome one or if he can pay up or not. You don't have to worry about his whims or his cracking you on the jaw or his inflamed genital tract. Nothing that happens will ever move you from the room, the bed, the darkness, and the sound of footsteps. The customers will keep coming and you'll keep being fed no matter what your hair looks like or what lies you think up to tell those wheezing over you, those without faces you can ever really see. It's peaceful, all right, in a 'still-life' house; and sometimes I wake up laughing at night thinking about it.

WALTER: I'll bet there were times, on a December night when business was slow on your corner, you felt such a place wouldn't be too bad.

LUCY: No. I liked the cold nights. Only the really interesting ones were out when the weather was mean. The ones who must have been like you were after your Gogarty trial.

WALTER: Can't you leave me out of it?

LUCY [*menacingly*]: Oh, you'd like to be left out of everything, wouldn't you? Everything but the Warden's filing cabinet.

WALTER: If you keep on this way, I'm going to have to ask you to leave.

LUCY [*moving towards him again*]: No chance of that, Walter. Too much depends on this for me. It's your world against mine. There'll be no 'still-life' house for Lucy because of you!

WALTER: Must we go through this again? I was through with everything you represent when the police took the blood-stained seven-iron out of my hand.

LUCY [*speaking evenly, with a smile, and still advancing*]: I don't believe you, Walter. All the talk about your little battle to keep the laws from crumbling after the Gogarty trial, I don't believe a word of it.

WALTER: Well, that's really beside the point.

LUCY [*reaching into her pocket, she brings out the packet of cigarettes and extracts several*]: Do you know what I believe, Walter? [*As she speaks, she begins throwing the cigarettes about the cell.*]

WALTER: Here, what are you doing?

LUCY [*flipping several over her shoulder*]: I'm setting up the atmosphere you really like.

WALTER [*dropping to his hands and knees to gather up the debris*]: Stop it! Stop it! I may not be able to find them all before they come for me.

LUCY [*walking now to the tray of food*]: Leave them, Walter. You don't mind a messy cell any more than you did finding yourself on the wrong trains. [*She opens the dish and extracts the chicken leg she'd already bitten into.*]

WALTER: What are you saying? It made me sick. It made me kill my wife. And put down that chicken bone!

LUCY: I think it would go well in the centre of the floor. A little savage bone in the centre of the cell. [*She throws the bone in the air and it lands with a clatter in the cell's centre.*] And maybe a wing in the corner. [*The piece of chicken bounces off the wall and drops in the cell's corner by the washbasin.*]

WALTER: I'm going to be hanged in an hour. How can you treat me this way?

LUCY: Yes, Walter, you were frightened of what those hiccups touched off, all right, but it was because you were starting to enjoy that dizzy world outside. That's why your wife had her head mashed, wasn't it? You just wanted to remove yourself from temptation.

WALTER [*no longer crawling about, but still on his hands and knees*]: That's not true! That's not true!

LUCY: Oh, come on, Walter. Weren't you beginning to look forward to those strange beds you turned up in?

WALTER [*protesting too much*]: No, they terrified me. I swear it!

LUCY [*seeing she has made a breach, she pushes on, speeding up her accusations*]: And your wife's birthmark – how many times did you bet with yourself where it would pop up next?

WALTER [*now breaking a bit*]: Once or twice only. But that doesn't mean . . .

LUCY: And how many snips at the dog's tail did you take?

WALTER: It was cruel, I know. But nothing seemed to matter in those days . . .

LUCY: And you enjoyed its howls.

WALTER: All my life I had an urge to torture a dog or cat. And it was just one snip. Just one!

LUCY: And when you went out at night, not knowing what tie you were wearing, what streets you were walking, what name you were using, admit you were twitching with excitement.

WALTER [*feebly*]: I won't; I wasn't.

LUCY [*going to the cot and picking up* WALTER'S *shirt*]: Admit it, or the number goes.

WALTER: I didn't, I swear I didn't.

[LUCY *rips the number-patch off in one short movement and* WALTER *cries as if he's been wounded. Then she holds the piece of cloth obtrusively in front of her and lets it drop slowly to the floor. Now totally defeated,* WALTER *watches it descend.*]

LUCY: Now the laws are falling apart again, Walter. You're just a numberless name about to be hanged. There's a not-so-bad-looking woman in your cell. What's there to lose? Do you remember having thoughts like these?

WALTER: Yes, yes, I had them. I thought for a time that all the springs, levers, and wheels of the world had broken down and I was free!

LUCY [*softening now*]: And so you were, Walter.

WALTER: No, there was too great a price. There were always those grey mornings when the mind took over, when you saw your crumpled clothes and cigarette pack from the night before, when your head pounded and you nibbled your lip in fear. Then you panicked for a world that made sense.

LUCY: No matter how much fun you got from the world that didn't?

WALTER: Oh, leave me alone.

LUCY [*helping* WALTER *to his feet*]: I'm going to bring that world back to you. After all, it's the only one there is.

WALTER [*weakly*]: There's my cell.

LUCY [*drawing him towards the cot*]: With the cigarettes on the floor? With the number torn from your shirt? With my perfume settling over you?

WALTER: Please, don't make me start again. What I found on those mornings was death; and it's only minutes away.

LUCY: Make love to me, Walter, and you won't mind the hangover of the gallows. You'll be living again when you strangle.

WALTER: That's no consolation! Oh, everything was so perfect here before you came. I was just like one of the Warden's insects, living out my days unconsciously, letting the fixed rhythms of the prison carry me along.

LUCY: It's too late to go back now. Look at the sky. How many stars are in your sections now?

WALTER: Why, they're all bunched in two or three of them, and the planet's gone entirely.

LUCY: And the cell, isn't it beginning to push in upon you?

WALTER: I loved it for so long.

LUCY: It's not big enough to hold a live man, Walter.

WALTER: Oh, why wasn't there a glass of water next to Mrs Gogarty in the courtroom? You would never have gotten to me then. I would have died somewhere in bed of a bad heart, thinking that a special chair had been set aside for me at an eternal dinner party where everything was properly served.

LUCY: No one's lucky enough to fool himself that way forever.

WALTER: But how can there ever be a contented expression on my face now when they come for me?

LUCY [*pulling him down onto the cot*]: Trust Lucy for that, Walter. All those nights, beds, marching songs, toothpaste containers, and howling dogs packed into thirty minutes.

WALTER: I hope so. Otherwise I think I'll break down and cry when I start up those steps.

LUCY: Shall we begin, Walter?

WALTER: All right, I've paid the price now. There'd better be twenty years of living in your mouth, fingertips, and breasts.

LUCY: I'll lead you, Walter. You just follow.

WALTER [*bending over her*]: And who knows? Maybe the rope will break? Or the hangman come down with a bad cold?

LUCY: That's the way to reason, Walter. On this cot, with Lucy on it, anything and everything's now possible. [*She draws* WALTER *to her and the cell's single light is extinguished.*]

CURTAIN

PART TWO

The curtain rises on the early morning confusion of a suburban kitchen-dining room. PHILLIP, *the prison's executioner, and* MARTHA, *his wife, are standing at the kitchen table.* PHILLIP *is a small, erect man. He is dressed in the trousers, shirt, and tie of his official uniform. The hat and coat are placed on one of the kitchen chairs. His wife, her hair in curlers and dowdily attractive in a morning housecoat, begins busying herself at the stove. A large red pepper mill is the only conspicuous object on the table.*

[*As the lights come up fully, the* WARDEN *is seen pacing back and forth across the table from* PHILLIP.]

WARDEN [*with rhetorical self-pity*]: When I think how I stayed up nights as a boy learning the penal code by heart so someday I would be a prison warden!

PHILLIP: What I asked for isn't going to prove you wasted your youth. It seems quite reasonable to me.

WARDEN: Reasonable? How can you, the last and most important link in society's chain of punishment, how can you think it reasonable to want to dress up like a headsman from the Middle Ages?

PHILLIP: I just want to wear a black hood over my head. I think it would lend me a little more – well, personality out there.

MARTHA [*setting a pot of coffee on the kitchen table*]: Well, if you ask me, the idea of a hood, especially a black one, strikes me as a little morbid.

WARDEN: There you are; from your wife. Can you imagine what others will have to say about it? Why, it smacks of thumbscrews, iron maidens, and unsanitary dungeons.

MARTHA [*to* PHILLIP]: I wish you'd come sit down and finish your oatmeal. [*Looking into one of the bowls set on the table*]

It's getting crusty and beginning to stick to the edges of the bowl.

PHILLIP [*a look of exasperation at* MARTHA]: I don't want any oatmeal now. I simply want, as an employee with some twenty years' service behind him, to have a request granted. [*With a little petulance*] I want to wear a black hood at today's execution!

WARDEN: But think of what it will do to your reputation! Instead of being a finely edged instrument in a clinical, detached operation, you become a villain – a strangler – a black knight.

MARTHA [*vigorously buttering a piece of toast*]: I can just imagine the treatment I'd get then from the girls in my bridge club.

PHILLIP: Let them jeer and hiss at me; it's better than not being noticed or thought of at all.

WARDEN: But behind a hood your face won't even be seen.

PHILLIP [*slightly angry*]: My face? Don't you think I know what this collection of scribbles, bumps, and creases looks like? Any real expression I call on it to take looks ridiculous on me. But with this hood, this mask, it comes alive. My eyes, outlined by slanting black slits, crackle with perception; my mouth grows full and moist; and my chin, as if obeying a command from these other features, squares itself and, just a little arrogantly, juts forward.

MARTHA [*now beginning to pour out three cups of coffee*]: It sounds as if you'd look like you were in a bad accident, Phillip.

WARDEN: I think you'd frighten the men to death before you had a chance to hang them.

PHILLIP: Then I would at least have some contact. [*A sigh.*] Oh, I didn't mind being your instrument when those condemned arrived like patients drowned in ether. But things have changed now. You yourself know that they come up those steps trembling, warm, talkative – exuding a scent so full of living that *my* head sometimes starts spinning because of it.

WARDEN: There are rules and regulations governing these things. An executioner's uniform can be blue, black, or grey; the buttons can be bone or brass; and the cap is optional. But by no stretch of interpretation is there any mention of a black hood.

PHILLIP: Hang the regulations! I'm trying to get a little colour into things. [*Pleading*] Don't you understand? I need a change.

WARDEN: You have your vacation coming up in a few months. Get in some fishing, and you'll feel better. I've always found that just dangling your line in a mountain stream relaxes the muscles, improves the digestion . . .

PHILLIP: I don't want to fish, Warden. For twenty years I've gone to little mountain streams on my vacation and caught nothing more interesting than a trout with one eye last summer.

WARDEN: A one-eyed trout? What kind of bait were you using?

PHILLIP: Don't change the subject. Now, do I or do I not wear my hood today?

WARDEN: I've already given you an answer on that.

PHILLIP: Just look at me in it, that's all. Just one glance.

WARDEN: I couldn't be less interested.

PHILLIP: All you have to say is yes or no. Just yes or no.

WARDEN [*giving in with a long sigh*]: It's a waste of time; but, if you want to, go ahead.

PHILLIP: Fine; it's just upstairs. [*Starting to leave*] Oh, I may be a little time adjusting it, though. It has to sit just right, otherwise it droops a bit and I find it difficult to breathe.

MARTHA: If you're just going to leave the oatmeal, should I have some scrambled eggs ready for you when you come down?

PHILLIP: Forget about breakfast, Martha. [*To the* WARDEN] I hope, once I'm in my hood, that I won't have to take it off until the ceremony's over with. I wouldn't want any food stains to get on it.

[PHILLIP *exits*.]

MARTHA: He used to eat such a big breakfast on special days like this. Why, I can remember when six eggs and a quarter-pound of ham were just enough for him.

WARDEN: Well, I must say I find his behaviour this morning

a little peculiar. The whole thing just isn't like Phillip.
He's always been someone you could count on, someone
who knew the importance of a good shine on his buttons
and a sharp crease in his trousers.

MARTHA [*sitting down dejectedly and absently stirring her coffee*]:
Well, something's definitely been happening to him in the
last months. If you'd been living with him every day, this
business with the hood wouldn't surprise you in the least.

WARDEN: I haven't noticed anything until now.

MARTHA: Oh, he's kept these changes fairly well hidden,
even from me. But you can't eat, sleep, and take out a
joint bank account with a man without noticing the slight-
est change in him.

WARDEN: Now that you mention it, he hasn't come to any
club meetings in the last months and his weekly reports
have been dotted with erasure smudges – very unlike him.

MARTHA [*putting the coffee down and nervously smoothing her hair*]:
It's beginning to show on the outside too? Oh, I'd hoped to
keep it confined to the rooms in this house.

WARDEN [*reaching down and taking* MARTHA'S *hand*]: Is it something you can tell me, a very old friend? Is there another
woman involved in all this?

MARTHA [*hitting the kitchen table with her free hand so that the*
WARDEN *turns the other loose*]: Oh, how I wish there was! How
I'd love to be able to sink my nails into the flesh-and-blood
reason for the way things are beginning to wobble on their
legs around here! Just to see a larger bosom or a firmer
behind leading Phillip down a street would let me spit at
him with a clear conscience. If I just knew where the weak-
ness was, I could make life miserable for him and then
forget it!

WARDEN: But you don't?

MARTHA [*rising from the kitchen table like a prosecutor at a trial*]:
About four months ago, after Phillip had left for work, I
got up from bed and, like I do every morning the first
thing, reached down for his slippers to take them to the
closet. For twenty years he's always left them on his side of
the bed, neatly placed next to one another, toes pointed to
the wall.

WARDEN: And that morning?

MARTHA: One was underneath the bed and the other, after being used for an ash tray, was tucked beneath his pillow.

WARDEN [*shaking his head*]: A bad sign!

MARTHA: Only the first, though. In the next weeks I began making all sorts of discoveries: in his bureau drawer, tucked among his underwear, I found a book of Swedish lessons; in the hall closet, squeezed behind the Christmas decorations, I uncovered a banjo with two of its strings missing; and under one of the sofa cushions, I turned up a pair of red socks with 'World's Fair – 1939' stitched down their sides. Red socks! I can't decide what to do with them, and just knowing they're sitting in the house drives me half out of my mind.

WARDEN [*approaching* MARTHA, *he puts his hands on her shoulders and speaks as the comforting male*]: Go on, Martha. My home's not a happy one, either.

MARTHA: Well, after that, Phillip himself began upsetting things. Since we were married, he's always slept on his stomach, one hand folded beneath his chin; but a month ago I woke up to find him snoring on his back. Then his favourite chair, that he always settled in after dinner, began being neglected; and, the dishes done, I'd come in and find him pouting in a corner or sitting cross-legged like an Arab on the floor.

WARDEN [*oozing sympathy*]: And you've been suffering through all this, Martha, without a word to anyone?

MARTHA: I kept hoping it would all pass over; but I see now it won't. Last night, behind a stack of bathroom towels, I discovered a box of very expensive cigars with an unpronounceable name – and then this morning the hood. [*She utters a long sigh and turns to put her head on the* WARDEN'S *chest.*] Oh, Warden!

WARDEN [*a smile hinting now a little more than sympathy*]: There, there. Please call me Harry.

MARTHA [*a brief smile as she pronounces the name*]: Harry! [*Now the defenceless little girl*] Oh, I just don't know what to do any longer.

WARDEN: I really can't stand thinking of you being unhappy.

MARTHA: Just last week Phillip refused to renew our country club membership or donate to the Red Cross.

WARDEN: You need help, Martha. Can Harry, an old, old, *old* friend, do anything for you?

MARTHA: Don't let him wear that hood today. No matter how he coaxes, put your foot down.

WARDEN [*a vigorous nod*]: You can depend on it. I'll simply tell him his pension won't be raised if he does.

MARTHA: Oh, Harry, you've always been so kind. Just having you here this morning makes everything seem much easier.

WARDEN [*lifting up her chin*]: We're cut from the same timber, Martha. Perhaps we can help each other. [*He starts to kiss her.*]

MARTHA [*pulling away*]: No, Harry! Even if Phillip has taken to collecting red socks and turning nasty remarks about my friends, I couldn't deceive him. It would be playing his game.

WARDEN: He does nothing but hurt you, Martha; and I've loved you ever since the day you came to my office to try to get a raise in salary out of me for Phillip.

MARTHA [*now enjoying being pursued*]: Really? I remember coming out feeling you hadn't noticed me at all. And Phillip didn't get the raise.

WARDEN: You were wearing an orange-and-blue print dress, white gloves and, as it was right after lunch, there was a little drop of mayonnaise on the left side of your chin.

MARTHA: Harry! And you didn't tell me.

WARDEN [*walking up to her and speaking in a hoarse voice*]: I found it terribly exciting. All the time you were going on about those extra five dollars a month, I was trying to imagine just what you could have eaten to put that tiny white mark there.

MARTHA [*pretending embarrassment*]: You shouldn't talk that way. What a woman eats for lunch is an intimate matter.

WARDEN: And you? Did you notice me at all?

MARTHA: I'd only been married six months at the time. I wasn't noticing anyone but Phillip, such that he was.

WARDEN [*somewhat hurt*]: You mean I made no impression at all?

MARTHA: Well, I do recall you had on a tie with a palm tree painted on it.

WARDEN [*nostalgically*]: In the dark it lit up and formed a pair of woman's legs.

MARTHA [*almost warmly*]: And I noticed how bloodshot your eyes were, and I thought how hard you must work to have popped so many of those little vessels.

WARDEN: Twenty years ago! Twenty years ago! If we could only have spoken frankly to each other then.

MARTHA: And why didn't you?

WARDEN: I thought of doing so, Martha. That very night I paced about in the dark of our five-room house, trying to decide just how bold I should be.

MARTHA: And then you saw your wife asleep, her head placed at just the right angle on the pillow, and you were ashamed of your thoughts. A good wife holds on even when she's unconscious.

WARDEN: Heavens no! It wasn't my wife. She'd already begun sampling the line of manual labourers that began with a teen-age elevator operator and just last week was kept going with a streetcar motorman. No, Martha, it was the twins, aged one, I think, at the time, who kept me from sending you a warm note about the stain on your chin. I wandered into their room, heard them breathing, in unison, and something made me switch on the light. I saw them: their eyes opened simultaneously, blinked once in disbelief at the questions written across my face, and gave me such a stare of clear-sighted respectability that I backed, shame-faced, from the crib. Oh, if you could have seen those accusing blue pupils daring me to jeopardize their owners' position. Martha, their plump faces were as solid as the walls of my prison, and they left me no choice but to forget your lunches and start saving for their college education.

MARTHA [*with a sigh of genuine understanding*]: Well, I don't blame you for that.

WARDEN: Oh, it was the right thing then when I thought you were happy with our hangman. But now . . .

MARTHA: Now, now it's too late. I can't put mayonnaise on my sandwiches any longer and fit into last year's dress.

WARDEN: And I wouldn't dare wear a tie with a palm tree painted on it. [*Suddenly throwing off the gloom that has settled over him and tumbling out his words*] But my sons are almost chemical engineers and my wife never stops riding streetcars and my house is empty and no matter what size dress you wear, I love you!

    [*He kisses* MARTHA *enthusiastically, and, for a moment, she returns in kind. Then, however, she pushes him away.*]

MARTHA: Oh, no, Harry. No, no, no. [*She walks back to the kitchen table and steadies herself with it.*] Let me re-heat your coffee or make you some toast.

WARDEN [*again advancing*]: Please, don't drop back behind breakfast. We're both beyond that now.

MARTHA [*again escaping*]: No, not here. Phillip may come down any minute.

WARDEN: Then we must have a meeting, a rendezvous as soon as possible. Twenty years, Martha. Twenty years!

MARTHA [*after a brief pause*]: All right: tomorrow, three o'clock, in front of the supermarket steps.

WARDEN: Tomorrow? [*A pause and a frown, as he consults a small black engagement book.*] No, I'm afraid tomorrow's out for me. A government inspection team is coming down for the day. [*Brightening*] But Saturday, in the afternoon, I know a little bar . . .

MARTHA: But I've promised myself as a fourth in three card games that afternoon.

WARDEN: Cards, Martha?

MARTHA [*with just a little less enthusiasm*]: We could try Monday morning. No one suspects you of anything on a Monday.

WARDEN [*a little impatient*]: That's because everyone's too busy to get into mischief. If I went away from my desk for five minutes after a weekend, it'd take me a month to catch up.

MARTHA: Well, I could slip away Tuesday night and say I'm seeing a movie.

WARDEN [*dejectedly*]: That's the night the twins call from school to ask for money. [*With now but faint hope*] But Wednesday?

MARTHA [*flatly, as she checks a calendar on the kitchen wall*]: Cancer Fund meeting. Thursday?

WARDEN [*in equally funereal tones*]: Parole Board all day, and I visit my mother at night.

> [MARTHA *turns and goes to the kitchen table where she pours a fresh cup of coffee. The* WARDEN *continues as though trying to explain something to himself rather than to her.*]

I've visited Mother every Thursday night since leaving her to get married. Every Thursday night, and I don't think she really enjoys seeing me at all.

MARTHA [*after a pause*]: Would you like cream in your coffee, Harry?

WARDEN: Black; make it as black as you can.

MARTHA [*making conversation*]: Do you suppose· it will rain? I always think hangings should take place in bad weather, even if it does make Phillip's back stiffen up a bit.

WARDEN [*taking up the coffee cup and staring moodily into it*]: Are we back to hangings, your husband, and another official day?

MARTHA: Your twins' eyes are still following us.

WARDEN [*putting down the cup*]: Ah, but for a moment, for a moment . . .

MARTHA [*sharply*]: We were being fools. Now drink your coffee.

WARDEN [*slinking around the table to her*]: At least one more kiss, Martha. The second and last one in twenty years.

MARTHA [*dryly*]: It would just be a wet sound to me now, Harry.

WARDEN: But not to me.

MARTHA: Your kiss would mean nothing but that I had to breathe through my nose for its duration.

WARDEN: And if I don't, I'll never breathe properly again. I feel as if I'm being sealed away forever in a very small hall closet.

MARTHA: And no matter what you do, I'll always be on the other side of the door. You won't even be near me, Harry.

WARDEN [*like a painful prayer*]: Oh, just this once let those damned chemical engineers look the other way!

> [*He begins kissing* MARTHA'S *neck passionately while she remains immobile. After a second,* PHILLIP, *his black hood over*

his head, enters. His voice, because of the mask, is somewhat muffled.]

PHILLIP: And just what is this going on?

[MARTHA *utters a cry and jumps back from the* WARDEN. *He turns around and is equally upset by what he sees.*]

WARDEN: Good God!

PHILLIP [*moving towards them*]: I'll ask again: what were you two doing?

WARDEN [*catching his breath and paying no attention to the question*]: Do you know how ridiculously ferocious you look? Your creeping in like that's sent a chill through me all the way down to my feet.

PHILLIP: Your feet? What do I care about your feet? You were kissing my wife.

WARDEN: What? That thing's covering your mouth and making it very hard to follow what you're excited about.

PHILLIP [*taking off the hood*]: I *say* you were kissing my wife!

WARDEN: It's not very well-mannered to come right out and say it that way, but I suppose I was.

PHILLIP: While I was upstairs, trying to adjust this hood so you'd see it to its best advantage, you were making love to my wife. You, the Warden of the prison, who, in less than half an hour will be raising a solemn forefinger and signalling me to hang a man – you were making love to my wife in my own kitchen.

WARDEN [*really confused by all the fuss*]: Man to man, Phillip, I apologize. These things happen all the time – a little slip that sets one in the bushes alongside somebody you've no business being in the bushes with. Yes, it's an unfortunate, uh, occurrence, and, as I said, I *do* apologize for it.

PHILLIP [*somewhat stunned*]: Apologize? Oh, no, please don't do that. I – I couldn't accept. I don't *want* to accept.

WARDEN: Now, Phillip, I understand how you feel. I've found my wife in much more than an embrace with a plumber. He was covered with grease, too, and had . . .

PHILLIP: Oh, no, it's not that at all. I was a little shocked just now and perhaps I did sound like a predictable husband. It just seemed that, under the circumstances, bellowing was expected of me.

WARDEN: I'm not following.

PHILLIP: It's simply that, while I was in my room, I was thinking what a failure I'd be in the hood. I was thinking, Harry, that the only thing that would save me would be to turn tail on this house, this uniform, this prison – everything that keeps me jogging along in step with the rest of you. So, Harry, friend and lover of my wife, I almost opened the window, slithered down the drainpipe and slipped out of your sight forever. I was going to run away – are you listening too, Martha? – run away and find out just where those men I've been dropping through gallows' doors come from.

WARDEN: Phillip, call me names, knock me down if you want to, but don't psychoanalyse yourself in public this way. At least not while you're in uniform.

PHILLIP: Let me just say that it was my old, well-trained conscience that kept me off the drainpipe. I thought of you two, standing firm on this dreary morning, washing your misery down with coffee, keeping to the rules of the game, and I bowed my head, covered it with the hood, and came downstairs ready to go on as Phillip, the old executioner. But now, now that you two have kicked up your heels a little bit, I see no reason why I shouldn't follow suit. You don't know how long I've waited to find a crack in the wall that being Martha's husband has built around me. But now that I see it's there, I'm going through it and down the drainpipe without a regret.

WARDEN: Phillip, this is all impossible, you know that, don't you?

PHILLIP: No more so than my finding you wrapped around my wife is impossible. If you two, at breakfast time, can stomach each other to the point of embracing, then I don't see how the line of impossibility can be drawn anywhere.

WARDEN: And just who, in all honesty, is responsible for this embrace?

PHILLIP [*looking at* MARTHA, *who, during the foregoing, has folded her arms and kept her back to both of her champions*]: Who, indeed?

WARDEN: You, yourself. You with your black hood, your Swedish lessons, your scattered slippers, and your brooding in the corner. You sent her into my arms, Phillip.

PHILLIP [*smiling at* MARTHA *who doesn't respond*]: So you did notice these things.

WARDEN: Of course she has; and that's why what happened happened. It explains . . .

PHILLIP: At five-thirty in the morning it doesn't explain . . .

WARDEN [*raising his arm for silence*]: No! No! I am now speaking in my official capacity and I don't want to be interrupted by subordinates. [*The* WARDEN *takes the deep breath of one preparing for platitudes.*] Life, Phillip, is like a long sea voyage – the comparison's an old but apt one. We begin by deciding whether we favour temperate, tropic, or arctic waters. We decide what ports to put into with proper ceremony and what savage islands to sell trinkets and contract diseases on. We select the style of ship and the type of crew that suits us; and if one turns out to have a few leaks hidden in its bottom and the other to be bad-breathed and mutinous, we don't let that force us to drift off course. For, Phillip, staying within the latitudes and longitudes we've marked out for ourselves is all that matters. There can be no floating about to take closer looks at a curvaceous coast line or a sensual horizon. There can be no seeking out restful doldrums when your nerves get a bit frayed or poking about for a good typhoon when calm seas prove somewhat tedious. No, we keep to the prescribed path, and when other ships plough past us, flaunting well-laundered sails – well, we scrub ours up too, send every one with scurvy out of sight, keep a good mile of sea water between us and our short-lived neighbours, and leave them with the impression of nothing but that we're occupying the exact bit of ocean marked out for us. But you, Phillip, you just weren't sticking to the chart. You were sailing into harbours that weren't even marked on the maps of your second-in-command; you were tossing sensible and costly cargo overboard to make room for unmarketable baubles; you were tilting the compass to suit yourself. Now, is there any wonder, as you were approaching the dangerous waters of middle age, that Martha should lower a dinghy over the side and paddle her way to a vessel that looked, at least from a distance, to be completely shipshape? And, of course, having a good set of sea manners and seeing your wife bobbing next to me, I took her aboard, gave her, so to speak, a change of dry clothes and am now ready to return her to your schooner which, I'm sure, will be polished up and made ready for inspection. And if you don't want her to think she has to abandon ship again, tighten the hatches, throw out your World's Fair socks; secure the rigging, don't use slippers for ash trays; scrub the decks, go to club dances; check your compass hourly, burn that revolting black hood; and, finally, appear at today's execution as if you knew what your co-ordinates as the state's official hangman were. For remember, Phillip, no matter how attractive you find the mermaids or the rocks they wrap their appealing green tails around, the important thing is to keep sailing on course. Take that as an old captain's advice – just keep sailing on course. [*The* WARDEN, *who during the speech has edged his way to the door, exits through it.*]

PHILLIP [*running to the door after him*]: That's the same speech you gave at the club's Christmas dinner last year and the summer picnic the year before! Well, you old pirate, you'd better get your ship's lifeboats ready because there isn't going to be a hanging today. Do you hear? The person you thought you temporarily rescued is now your permanent passenger. I resign! From everything! I resign! [PHILLIP *pauses for a moment, comes back into the centre of the kitchen, looks at his hood, then at* MARTHA, *and laughs softly.*] I'll have to admit you surprised me, Martha. It was pleasant, but a surprise nevertheless. [*Silence.*] Well, don't you have anything to say? After all, I just said I was leaving you.

MARTHA [*disinterested*]: If you're not going to touch breakfast, I'll put the dishes away.

PHILLIP [*relieved*]: Oh, I thought after twenty years of marriage that a little piece of flesh had begun to sprout, connecting us together like Siamese twins. You don't know how upset I was by the idea. And now, Martha, you've shown me that it's nothing but a flimsy band-aid – nothing more.

MARTHA [*beginning to remove the dishes and wash them*]: A band-aid?

PHILLIP [*with real admiration in his eyes*]: One that you had the courage to tear off. Oh, if I'd only known how simple it would be. There I was, trying to sneak into a black hood and leave little hints about the house.

MARTHA: Hints at what?

PHILLIP: Hints that I was unhappy; that I thought I'd become little more than the brass and flannel of my uniform; that I wanted to run away from everything that I was and had been. It never occurred to me that you might feel the same way. But then, seeing you pressed up against the Warden – well, Martha, I confess I underestimated you.

MARTHA: And are you planning now to go out and make love to the Warden's wife?

PHILLIP: Oh, no. I'm going to leave you and this little piece of the world forever. I'm going to become – to become . . .

MARTHA [*sharply*]: What?

PHILLIP [*a visionary smile*]: To become – to become something like those fellows I've been hanging in the last few months. Do you know, Martha, there's a light in their eyes, a pulse behind their ear that beats faster than mine, and an interest in the weather that makes me envy them. Oh, they're frightened all right, but it's a healthy fear – something I don't think I would ever have had.

MARTHA: As the Warden said, they've just left those official ladies. Maybe if you didn't read all night in bed we could . . .

PHILLIP: Oh, no, Martha. I need a complete and total break.

MARTHA: And when do you plan to start breaking?

PHILLIP: In the past a step like this would have meant travel folders, reservations, exact calculations down to the dollar. But now, Martha, I'm not even going to bother to pack. I'm walking straight out the door without a glance over my shoulder.

MARTHA [*holding out a plate to him*]: Will you help dry first?

PHILLIP [*abstracted but pleasant*]: What? Oh, certainly. [*Towel and plate in hand, he goes back to his vision.*] First, I'm going to a tailor. I'm going to have him make me something for every mood I'm going to try – silk vests, lace collars, green tweeds for reflective moments . . .

MARTHA [*handing him another dish*]: Tweeds always make you break out in a rash.

PHILLIP [*thinking for a moment, he takes the new plate and stacks the old one*]: That's true. Well, perhaps, I'll give up reflection – there won't be much time for it, I hope, anyway.

MARTHA: And after the tailor, then what?

PHILLIP: Ah, I want to go where the climate's very hot; where it steams, as a matter of fact; where oversized plants seem to couple with one another before your eyes and produce offspring so colourful that they look indecent.

MARTHA [*now a cup in her hand*]: You never liked me to wear loud clothes: always grey, black, and brown.

PHILLIP [*taking the cup*]: No offence, but you're just not a tropical plant, Martha.

MARTHA: It wasn't me who had to have an air-conditioner last summer. Put the cup face down, Phillip.

[*He does so and receives a bowl in its place.*]

PHILLIP: Now I want the heat to prevent anything from taking on too solid and sensible a shape. I want everything about me to shimmer, sway, and change in a second's time as if it were all one big sleight-of-hand trick. People, too, should melt and harden in front of you. [*He starts to put the bowl away.*]

MARTHA: That still looks wet to me.

PHILLIP [*retrieving the bowl*]: And, Martha, there might be mirages. Can you imagine, scenes floating about purely for your own amusement. Do you know, I think I've wanted to see a mirage for the last ten years.

MARTHA: You're getting water on your trousers, Phillip. [*She opens a cupboard and takes out an apron.*] Here, put this on.

PHILLIP [*getting into the apron*]: I used to try to force a mirage on myself. On days like today, when I'd see the man I was to hang being escorted toward me, I used to widen my eyes, clench my fists, and try to make my brain turn the entire scene into something else. It never worked, though: my eyes would begin to water and soon I was receiving reprimands from my superiors for what they took to be my emotional attitude while on duty.

MARTHA [*handing* PHILLIP *the last dish*]: All you want, then, is to see mirages?

PHILLIP: I want my pores to open and let out of me all the bubbling perspiration that's been stopped up by the civil service code. Think of it, Martha! Me, in the middle of a jungle, where everything's raw and fresh, where only the hungry and alive do the executing, where . . .

MARTHA: I think some grounds are still in the coffee-pot.

PHILLIP [*giving the pot another rinse*]: And then, Martha, once I've filled my lungs with that wild air – well, then I'll be ready to – to . . .

MARTHA: To what, Phillip?

PHILLIP [*modestly, with some embarrassment*]: Oh, grow a beard perhaps.

MARTHA: All this trouble just to avoid shaving?

PHILLIP: No, what I mean is, once I've finally shed this old skin, I'll be ready to – to take up my old profession again with a fresh hand.

MARTHA: You mean after all that sweating in the tropics you'd still want to be an executioner?

PHILLIP [*soberly*]: That is my profession, my trade, the only thing I can do passably well. [*Brightening*] But, Martha, I won't be an official piece of cloth and brass, tying the knot around living necks because someone, somewhere, has underlined their names in red ink.

MARTHA [*as if humouring someone not too sound of mind*]: You're going to do free-lance work?

PHILLIP [*slowly winding the dish-towel into a strangling cord*]: I'm going to have an eye peeled for all the dead branches that need pruning – for all those who want to measure away the few wild patches of weeds left to us and turn the ground, teeming with savage centipedes, into a middle-income housing development.

MARTHA [*still indulging him*]: And just how do you go about determining when a branch is dead?

PHILLIP [*moving about the kitchen table, towel in hand and eyes agleam*]: Oh, that won't be hard, Martha. [*He begins circling the table, his eyes on the pepper mill as if stalking it.*] Just suppose I'm standing on a busy corner at lunchtime. Oh, there'll be a lot of dead wood about, but I'll find the one beyond the help of insecticides. I'll know him: perhaps I'll notice that his tie, socks, and handkerchief match; or perhaps I'll see he doesn't cross the street until the exact moment the light blinks in his favour. Oh, I'll know him as one of those who'll spend what energy he has trying to make tomorrow a line-for-line copy of yesterday; one of those who has a favourite chair, who sees no difference but age between the woman he married and the woman he keeps. [PHILLIP *pauses, narrows his eyes, and moves in on the pepper mill.*] He won't notice me, but I'll be behind him all the time. I'll watch him stuff himself with just the right calorie count; I'll smile as he leaves the proper tip and takes the long way back to his office to get in a little exercise; I'll peek around a corner as he tells an off-colour joke to his secretary and pats her knee. And then, when he's alone in his office, about to balance another day's equation, I'll just tiptoe up behind him, hold the loop for a moment over his head, and then – snap! [*He catches the pepper mill in the towel's knot and lifts it up level with his eyes.*] There won't be any struggle or sound. He might have just enough curiosity to turn and see just who's doing him in, but the only thing I'd find in his eyes would be the gleam of one whose funeral arrangements were planned down to the last flower, tear, and comma in his epitaph. Already dead, Martha, he'd be only too happy to lie down. [PHILLIP *lets the pepper mill drop to the floor.*]

MARTHA [*getting down to retrieve it*]: That pepper mill was your birthday gift from my mother!

PHILLIP [*as if suddenly startled awake*]: What?

MARTHA [*putting the object back on the kitchen table*]: It must have cost twenty-five dollars. [*Sharply*] Find something less expensive to play games with, Phillip.

PHILLIP [*hurt*]: Games? Martha, I was trying to share a secret with you. For the first time in our marriage, I was telling you something I really felt.

MARTHA: Don't be open-hearted and frank with me, Phillip.

PHILLIP: But aren't you at least interested in what I'm really like?

MARTHA: If I was interested in what you were really like, I don't think I'd have stayed married to you for twenty years.

PHILLIP: But you might find me – well, exciting.

MARTHA [*coldly*]: I've grown used to the lies, Phillip. They make up the comfortable husband I know.

PHILLIP [*realizing he's made a mistake in confiding in her*]: Oh, I see. All right, then, you keep the comfortable husband! The new one, Martha, won't bother you any longer. No, he's simply going to close his eyes, turn around, and head straight through the door.

[*As he speaks,* PHILLIP *performs the above gestures. As he is halfway to the door, however,* MARTHA *speaks up.*]

MARTHA: You'd better take off my apron first.

PHILLIP [*angry with himself for not having noticed it*]: Oh, yes. How did I get into it in the first place?

MARTHA [*as if she were discussing a shopping list*]: And another thing: I don't see how you can pick up and leave today, Phillip.

PHILLIP [*repeating the above gestures*]: And why not, Martha? Why shouldn't I just close my eyes, turn around, and . . .

MARTHA: Because you have a dentist appointment first thing tomorrow morning.

PHILLIP [*turning about in confusion*]: Dentist? Dentist?

MARTHA [*innocently*]: You remember. The molar in the back has to come out? It's infecting the gum? Because of it you can't eat sweets?

PHILLIP: I don't want to eat sweets. I just . . .

MARTHA: We've been invited to my sister's for dinner Friday, and you know how partial you are to her chocolate mousse.

PHILLIP [*at last rather angry*]: Damn the chocolate mousse! I'm not going to your sister's for dinner anyway.

MARTHA: I've already accepted. And with the weekend whirl coming up, I don't see how you can plan to leave before next Wednesday.

PHILLIP: Plan? Something like this can't be planned and put on schedule. I'm giving up knowing where and what I'll be a week, a day, or even an hour ahead. I'm going to be . . .

MARTHA [*again sharp and bitter*]: A man-eating, jungle plant –
I know. Well, you'll have to wait until *after* my sister's
dinner to start blooming. And by that time, there'll be
other things popping up to detain you.

PHILLIP [*a little unnerved*]: Martha, maybe you didn't understand or listen to what I was saying. I'm sweeping all the
old laws, manners, and invitations under the rug. There's
nothing here that can hold me now.

MARTHA: Oh, yes, there is – me.

PHILLIP: You? Martha, I don't want to be brutal, but if
nothing else were pushing me through that door, you, in
your breakfast face, would be all the reason I'd need.

MARTHA [*now in full attack*]: Maybe my face won't charm you
into bed, but you're going to look at it, speak to it, and –
yes, even kiss it in a businesslike way every day of your life.
Because, Phillip, covered with cold-cream or skin oil, it's
the face of your wife. And 'wife', Phillip, means a thousand
obstacles for you to get over before you're free to start
chopping down dead branches.

PHILLIP [*in the tones of family argument*]: Wife? Hah! And were
you my wife with the Warden pawing over you?

MARTHA: More than ever, Phillip. That little moment with
him only reminded me how snug I was with you – even with
your red socks under the sofa seat. My life depends on all the
little functions you perform. You're like the telephone,
electricity, or underground plumbing. My life takes you for
granted, but would be lost without you. Maybe we're not
held together by a little piece of flesh, but there is something
there even harder to snip apart. It's the word 'and' in
'man *and* wife'. It's official and keeps us together through
mistresses, dreams, bills, and burned toast. 'Man *and* wife' –
that's our world, Phillip; and everything in it has long
ago been discovered, named, and placed in its proper
corner.

PHILLIP: No three-letter word's going to drag me after it.
Not when I finally have the chance . . .

MARTHA: You *had* the chance, Phillip. For the briefest second,
when you caught the Warden and me, you had the chance.
But no; you stayed and helped me with the dishes.

PHILLIP: That was just habit.

MARTHA: No, dear, that was the law of gravity yanking you right back to earth.

PHILLIP: Well, I'm breaking the law of gravity, Martha. From now on you'll have to find someone else to eat off and dry your dishes. The first day of creation is waiting for me on the other side of the kitchen door, and all the rules of marriage or physics aren't going to keep me from it. [*He starts for the door.*]

MARTHA: Touch that door and you'll find out how unpleasant the truth about yourself can be.

PHILLIP: I have all the truth I need, Martha. Good-bye. And if we ever meet again be careful I don't mistake you for a dead branch. [PHILLIP *makes to open the door, but finds it refuses to budge. He begins tugging at the knob.*] It must be the dampness has made the wood swell.

MARTHA [*taunting*]: You'll never get it open, Phillip. You know too well what's on the other side.

PHILLIP [*increasing his efforts*]: It's not locked. There's no reason for it to be this stubborn.

MARTHA: You don't want to strain yourself, Phillip. Remember that awful rubber girdle you had to wear after cleaning out the attic last year.

PHILLIP [*more and more effort*]: Shut up, Martha!

MARTHA: Ha! Don't yell at *me*! You, I, and the door know on which side of it you belong.

PHILLIP [*losing all control*]: I'll tear the damned thing off its hinges.

MARTHA: That door's the speed of light – a permanent boundary fence. It can't be broken.

PHILLIP [*now pounding on the door*]: Open, damn you! Open!

MARTHA: It won't because you don't want it to. You know that all your jungle will give you is athlete's foot, diarrhoea, and swollen joints.

PHILLIP [*turning from the door to* MARTHA, *he pleads with desperation in his voice*]: I'm going to tear down every kitchen door in the world. I'm going to strangle, murder . . .

MARTHA: You, murder? Hah! Come on, Phillip, the game's over. You're an official executioner, a little paunchy through the middle, with thinning hair and an obedient attitude. That's as close as you'll ever be to a murderer.

PHILLIP [*menacingly*]: If that door doesn't open you'll be the first to know how wrong you are.

MARTHA [*with an incredulous smile*]: Are you threatening me?

PHILLIP: If you're keeping me in this kitchen – yes!

MARTHA: Oh, poor, poor Phillip. Look at you; out of breath already and not even one step away from the house yet.

PHILLIP: I won't stand you laughing at me!

MARTHA: Then don't make jokes about doing me in. You're not on your gallows now; no twenty-five forms have been filled out in triplicate authorizing you to snap my neck. [*Shouting*] You're my husband! And that makes you the most harmless person in the world as far as *I'm* concerned!

PHILLIP [*picking up the black hood from the kitchen table and beginning to knot it ominously*]: For the last time: make the door open!

MARTHA: How can I, Phillip? You're the one who's keeping it shut. If you really wanted to leave, it would spring open like a hungry mouth.

PHILLIP [*stepping towards her*]: Then I'll have to prove I'm in earnest, Martha.

MARTHA: Don't be an ass. One of the things that will make the rest of our life together tolerable is that you can keep your mind buzzing with plans to murder me. Don't try it now and find out you can't. It'll make you sour, bitter, and even more difficult to get new hats and dresses out of than you are now.

[PHILLIP *begins testing the hood's strength and continues his advance.*]

MARTHA [*quite earnestly*]: I'm warning you. With as much love as I can squeeze out of me after twenty years, I'm warning you not to do this to yourself.

PHILLIP: As the books say: there's no good reasoning with a murderer.

MARTHA [*throwing back the challenge*]: All right, murderer, if you won't listen–. [*She picks up one of the kitchen table chairs, places it down-stage, facing the audience, and sits in it with her neck thrust out as if for a sacrifice.*] All right then, go ahead. Try and squeeze the air out of my windpipe. Just try it! Well, what are you waiting for, Bluebeard? Come on, let me feel some of your jungle sweat dripping down the back of my neck.

PHILLIP [*a little startled by* MARTHA's *action*]: Are you just going to sit there as if you were having your hair done?

MARTHA: You'll have to supply the noise and screams, Phillip. I'm just going to sit here and talk.

PHILLIP: Talk? Then that's just the last bit of incentive I need. [*He knots the hood around* MARTHA's *neck and begins tightening.*]

MARTHA [*not affected at all by* PHILLIP's *attack*]: Oh, you'll have to pull harder than that. I'm still getting in more than enough air to tell you that the ivy plants over our bed are all the jungle you'll ever know.

[PHILLIP *gives an extra hard tug, and* MARTHA *starts, as if tickled.*]

And it's your turn to water them next week. You'll take care of them every other week for as long as you're on this planet.

PHILLIP [*hopefully*]: Is the blood beginning to pound in your head? Do you find it difficult to focus your eyes?

MARTHA: Hah! I've never felt better. This is the closest we've come to sex in years.

PHILLIP [*increasing his efforts*]: And now, Martha, is your past popping up in front of you?

MARTHA: Only my future. And you, Phillip, growing stooped, absent-minded, and a little sloppy at the table, are in every minute of it.

PHILLIP [*becoming frustrated*]: You should at least be gagging now, damn it!

MARTHA [*sweetly*]: I don't know how to gag. But I could cough a little if it would make things easier for you.

PHILLIP [*pleading*]: Please stop breathing, Martha. Please, my arms are getting tired – please stop breathing.

MARTHA: At this rate, you'll stop before I will. Oh, what a story this will make at cards Saturday!

PHILLIP [*makes one last supreme effort, and then, with a groan, drops his hands*]: I just can't do it. My wrists and fingers just aren't strong enough. [*He sits in one of the kitchen chairs.*] I can't even get out of the kitchen.

MARTHA [*rubbing her neck and rising from the chair*]: I told you, Phillip, but you wouldn't listen, would you? Now look at you – panting and overheated. [*She takes the hood and begins mopping his brow.*] And you have to go out right away. I'm sure this will mean a cold by tomorrow.

PHILLIP [*docilely*]: Go out?

MARTHA: There's not fifteen minutes till the execution begins. There now, that's the best I can do. [*She takes* PHILLIP'S *coat and holds it out for him.*] All right, come on, get into this. If you keep all the buttons closed there's still a chance I won't have to spend a fortune on nose drops and cough syrup.

PHILLIP: So the execution's going to take place after all?

MARTHA [*buttoning up the coat*]: Of course it is; and you're going to be on those gallows, stiff and tall, the way I, the Warden, and the man you're going to hang expect you to be. The whole thing will go very smoothly now, won't it?

PHILLIP: I suppose it will.

MARTHA [*finishing the buttoning,* MARTHA *steps back to admire her work*]: There! Now you look like my husband and the state's official executioner. You can tell at a glance that you're a fish in the right waters now.

PHILLIP: I guess you can.

MARTHA [*picking up* PHILLIP'S *cap*]: Now, don't be so gloomy. Look on the bright side of everything to come. Think of the certificate of merit and pension bonus you'll receive when you successfully hang your thousandth man. Think of the speeches you'll be asked to give to college students on the fine prose in the penal code. Think of the jokes you'll tell at your retirement dinner and the little cottage our insurance policy's going to give us. Think how peaceful things will be when you're certain that there's only one world and one way to live in it.

PHILLIP: Will that come with the retirement policy too?

MARTHA [*putting the cap on his head*]: It just might, Phillip. It just might. And now, you're complete; not a wrinkle in you. [*She takes his arm and starts to lead him towards the door.*]

PHILLIP: My hood? Can I at least have that?

MARTHA: I'll put it under the sofa with your socks. And, on holidays, you can take them, your banjo, and the other things out to look at for a while. And on New Year's Eve, you can even sit on the floor and flip ashes into your slippers if you want to.

PHILLIP: I think I'll go back to my chair. The floor's very hard.

MARTHA: That *is* more sensible, I suppose.

[*They reach the door.*]

Well, come on now. Out you go.

PHILLIP: But it won't open.

MARTHA [*she touches the door knob ever so lightly with the tips of her fingers and it springs open*]: There's nothing holding it shut now.

PHILLIP [*taking a step towards the opening*]: It is very cold this morning.

MARTHA: Do you have a handkerchief with you?

PHILLIP [*feeling his pocket*]: Yes.

MARTHA: Well, then, you'd better be off.

PHILLIP [*turning towards* MARTHA]: Martha, I just wanted to be . . .

MARTHA: But you couldn't, Phillip. Some things just can't be broken. So you'd better just try to keep warm out there and forget all about it. Now, kiss me good-bye.

PHILLIP: But isn't there any chance for me at all?

MARTHA [*in a command voice and pointing to her cheek*]: Kiss!

[PHILLIP *does so, and then slowly turns and leaves.* MARTHA *waits for a moment and then calls out to him.*]

Keep bundled up, dear. Don't work too hard. And tonight – tonight we'll have something very special for dinner. Something you really like, dear, something you really, really like.

CURTAIN

MURRAY SCHISGAL

THE TYPISTS

To Reene

PREFACE

PASSING through London on the way to Spain a few summers ago, I gave, without much optimism, three short plays I had written (*The Typists* and *The Tiger* were among them) to a small theatrical group that worked at the British Drama League. Almost at once I was told that they would be produced. This came as quite a surprise. Until then I had never seriously thought of the European theatre as being essential, psychologically as well as practically, to the American playwright.

The plays were done and I came back to New York, without ever having reached Spain. Within two weeks I was called back to London. *The Typists* was taped for British television, productions at the Edinburgh Festival and in Israel were arranged. While in London this second time, Michael Codron and David Hall, producers, took an option on a long play of mine. I returned to New York, finished another play, *Ducks and Lovers*, and sent it off to them. They decided to do this play instead of the other, and once again I returned to London. *Ducks and Lovers* was produced at the Arts Theatre in December 1961. I returned home. A month later I was back in London, writing the scenario of *Ducks and Lovers* for an English movie company. And while in London this fourth time, Oscar Lewenstein took an option on my latest play, *Luv*.

My experience is not, I'm sure, so very unique. What is unique is the knowledge that American playwrights are beginning to share: the knowledge that the European theatre is more valuable to him in certain instances than the theatre at home. This is particularly true if he is a newcomer or if his play brings forth the shibboleth of 'commercial feasibility'. I find none of this dismaying. A bit peculiar, perhaps.

MURRAY SCHISGAL

First presented professionally by *In-Stage* in November 1960
at the British Drama League Studio-Theatre

CAST

PHILIPPA REID
LEONARD FENTON

Directed by *Charles Marowitz*

Time: At twenty-odd years of age.

Scene: An office: forward, centre, a pair of simple metal typewriter tables, with leaves extended, on which there are two old standard typewriters, stacks of postcards, and a bulky telephone directory on each; rear, a large window, two tall green steel file cabinets, a desk between them on which there are a great many telephone directories and a telephone, a door to the rest-room; at the right wall, forward, a water cooler, a wooden coat hanger, the entrance door; in the left wall, the door to the employer's office.

The sun streams through the window; as the play progresses it fades imperceptibly until, at the end, the room is almost in complete darkness.

The same clothes are worn throughout by the actors, although altered to suit the physical changes – subtle, almost unnoticed when they occur – that take place during the course of the play.

[SYLVIA PAYTON *enters from right. She is late for work. She throws her coat on the hanger, rushes across the room, deposits her lunch bag in the top drawer of a cabinet, removes cover from her typewriter and begins typing rapidly, glancing anxiously at the employer's door. In a moment she relaxes; she types slowly and hums to herself; she takes her comb and mirror from her pocketbook and fixes her hair. The front door opens. She puts everything away and without turning to see who has entered she starts to type rapidly again.* PAUL CUNNINGHAM *approaches, passing his lunch bag from hand to hand.*]

PAUL: Good morning. I'm Paul Cunningham. I was hired yesterday by... [*Laughing uneasily*] That's funny. I forgot his name. You'll have to excuse me. First day on the job. . . .

I'm a little nervous. It was the boss who hired me, though; at least that's what he said.

SYLVIA: I know. He told me. [*Rising, shaking his hand*] Sylvia. Miss Sylvia Payton. Glad to meet you, Mr Cunningham. If you'll hang up your coat I'll show you what you have to do.

PAUL: I'm sorry I'm late, Miss Payton. I got on the wrong train by mistake. Generally you'll find that I'm a pretty prompt person.

SYLVIA: Oh, that's all right. Just make sure it doesn't happen too often. He's very strict when it comes to being here on time. And now that he's made me responsible for this whole department. . . . Of course I won't say anything to him about this morning.

PAUL: I'd appreciate that a lot.

SYLVIA: Don't even mention it. Believe me, I didn't ask him to be made a supervisor. I don't like telling anyone what to do; that's part of my nature, I guess. You give me your lunch bag, Mr Cunningham. I'll put it in the file cabinet; that's where I keep mine.

PAUL: Thanks. I was sure lucky to get this job. I go to school at night and a lot of firms don't hire you if they know that.

SYLVIA: You must be a very ambitious person. What are you studying?

PAUL [*proudly*]: Law. Another three years and I should get my degree. Boy, that's one day I'm looking forward to.

SYLVIA: It must be extremely difficult to have a job and go to school at the same time.

PAUL: It's been real rough so far. But it has its advantages. When I get out, I'm going to have the satisfaction of knowing I did it myself, with my own sweat and my own money; that's more than most fellows my age can say.

SYLVIA: How true that is.

PAUL: Listen, I have an uncle who's a lawyer, a pretty darn famous lawyer, too. Francis T. Cunningham. You ask anybody in the legal field about Francis T. Cunningham and they'll tell you how much he's worth. Well, if I wanted to, I just have to pick up that phone, give him a ring and my worrying days would be over. But that's not for me; no, sir. I'll do it alone or I'm not doing it at all.

SYLVIA [*uncovers* PAUL'S *typewriter, opens directory for him*]: I think you're a hundred per cent right. You know, I once went with a boy – it was nothing serious, it could have been, but . . . I won't go into that now. Anyway, his father was helping him through medical school. He didn't have to earn a penny of his own. Do you think he finished? What happened was that his father remarried and stopped giving him money. He fell completely apart; you never saw anything like it.

PAUL: There's no substitute for character.

SYLVIA: That's exactly the point. Well, we'd better get to work before he starts screaming. We're on a promotion campaign now and it's a very important job. I suppose that's why you were hired. What we do is type out the names and addresses of prospective customers on these postcards. The advertisement is printed on the back. We get the information we want straight from the telephone book. Don't leave out any names; go right down the line. He checks everything and he can be awfully mean if he wants to. I've just started on the A's, so you'll start with the . . .

PAUL: B's.

SYLVIA: Right. That way we'll be sure to get everyone.

PAUL: It sounds easy enough.

SYLVIA: It is. And after awhile you can do it without even thinking.

[*They are both seated, typing.*]

PAUL: Ooops! My first card and my first mistake. I'm afraid I'm a little rusty. I haven't been doing much typing lately. [*He is about to throw card into basket.*]

SYLVIA: No, don't throw it away. If he sees it, he'll raise the roof. At the beginning you ought to type more slowly. Lean back in your chair. Posture's very important. And strike each key with the same steady rhythm.

PAUL: Like this?

SYLVIA: Better, much better; don't move your head; keep your eyes on the material you're typing.

PAUL [*sitting rigidly, uncomfortably*]: It's really nice of you to help me this way.

SYLVIA: I'm only too glad to, Mr Cunningham.

PAUL: Paul.

SYLVIA [*staring at him, warmly*]: Paul.

    [*The buzzer rings once.*]

That's for me. [*Quickly tidying herself*] He doesn't usually call me in this early. You go on with your work, Paul. He gets furious when he doesn't hear these typewriters going. He probably wants to know why it took us so long to get started this morning. Don't worry. I'll cover up for you.

PAUL [*holding her arm*]: Thanks for everything, Sylvia.

SYLVIA: You're welcome . . . Paul.

    [*Paul watches her as she swings her hips self-consciously and exits to employer's office. He then starts to type, makes an error, crumples card and is about to throw it into basket; on second thought he slips the card into his pocket. Again he types and makes an error, looks guiltily towards the employer's office and slips card into his pocket. All the while he whistles to the tune of 'Way Down Upon The Swanee River . . .'.*]

SYLVIA [*entering angrily*]: He's got some goddamn nerve! What does he think I am, a child? I see it doesn't pay to be nice to people. Well, he can just go and look for someone else to do his dirty work. I'm leaving! [*Gathers her things together.*]

PAUL: What happened?

SYLVIA: Bawling me out for being five minutes late; that's nerve, believe me.

PAUL [*laughing*]: So you were late this morning, too?

SYLVIA: There's nothing funny about it, Paul. When you've devoted as much time and energy as I have to this firm, giving them the best you're capable of, then maybe you'll see things differently. Where are my gloves?

PAUL [*rising, gives them to her*]: Here they are. Listen, Sylvia; you're excited. Why don't you think about it, huh?

SYLVIA: There's nothing to think about. When he asks you where I went, you just tell him for me that I don't care to associate with a firm that has no feelings for its employees. [*She struggles with coat; he helps her put it on.*]

PAUL: It's not easy finding a job now, I can tell you that.

SYLVIA: With my experience? You must be joking. I've been made many many offers in the past that I've refused out of a sense of loyalty to that . . . to that sex maniac in there. This is my reward.

PAUL: I wouldn't give him the satisfaction; no, sir.

SYLVIA: What satisfaction?

PAUL: Well, it stands to reason that he wanted you to quit, doesn't it? He knows you're a sensitive girl. By leaving you're doing just what he wants.

SYLVIA: You think he deliberately . . .

PAUL: Why else would he have bawled you out?

SYLVIA [*slight pause; takes off coat, puts it on hanger*]: I'd die before I gave him the satisfaction. If that's what he has in mind, he's got another guess coming. I'm leaving at my convenience, not his.

PAUL: Now you're talking.

SYLVIA: Believe me, there'll come a day when he'll really need me. 'Miss Payton, won't you please help me get this job through in time?' Then it'll be my turn. I'll just laugh right in his stupid face and walk out.

PAUL: Boy, I'd like to be here to see it. Is he married?

SYLVIA: Who would marry him? Ugly as sin, that's what he is.
    [*They type, laugh over the noise of their typing, then suddenly stop.*]

SYLVIA: We had a girl working here once; she was a riot. She used to draw these caricatures and mail them to him; anonymously, of course. But you should have seen them; they were the funniest thing.
    [*They type, laugh, stop suddenly.*]

PAUL: The last job I had was for this woman, Mrs Jameson. She was as blind as a bat without her glasses. You know what we used to do? Whenever we got the chance we hid her glasses somewhere in the office. For two or three days until she'd find them, we didn't have to do anything, not a single piece of work. We just sat around talking all day.

SYLVIA: I was with an insurance company when I graduated from high school. There was this man in charge there, Mr Williams, his name was, and he used to have loose hands, if you know what I mean.

PAUL: I know.

SYLVIA: Well, one day he was telling me how to type a policy and he let his hands fall – very, very casually – on my shoulder. So I turned around and looked up at him and spat right in his face.

PAUL: You were fired, I bet.

SYLVIA: As a matter of fact we got along very well after that.

[*They type; stop suddenly; turn to one another.*]

PAUL: Have you read any good books lately?

SYLVIA: I read a very good detective novel last week. It was called *Murder in Bombay*.

PAUL: I'm a science fiction man myself.

[*They type; stop suddenly; turn to one another.*]

SYLVIA: Can I ask you something?

PAUL: Sure. What is it?

SYLVIA: If you had to choose between getting a million dollars or losing a leg which would you take?

PAUL: Right leg or left leg?

SYLVIA: Any leg.

[*Pause.*]

PAUL: I'd take the million dollars.

SYLVIA: I wouldn't. I'd keep my legs.

[*They type; stop suddenly. They both stare at the audience,* PAUL *leaning forward,* SYLVIA *back in her chair, her face expressionless, her hands in her lap.*]

PAUL: I was born in a poor section of Brooklyn. My parents were at each other's throat most of the time. It was a miserable childhood. I had no brothers or sisters; there was only the three of us living in this old run-down house, with cats crying and screaming all night in the alley. Why my parents ever got married, I don't know, and why they stayed together for as long as they did I don't know that either. They're separated now. But it doesn't much matter any more. They were as unlike as any two people could be. All my father wanted was to be left alone to smoke his pipe and listen to the radio. My mother – she was a pretty woman, she knew how to dress, all right – she liked to go out and enjoy herself. I was stuck between the two of them and they pulled on both sides. I couldn't talk to one without the other accusing me of being ungrateful; I couldn't touch or kiss one of them without being afraid that the other one would see me and there would be a fight. I had to keep my thoughts to myself. I had to grow up wishing for some kind of miracle. I remember coming home from school one afternoon. I must have been twelve or thirteen. There was this man in the living-room with my mother. They weren't doing anything; they were just sitting and talking. But I felt that something was going on. I seemed to stop breathing and I ran out of the house and threw up on the kerbstone. Later on I swore to myself that I would make a miracle happen; that I wouldn't ever have to be where I didn't want to be and I wouldn't have to do what I didn't want to do; that I could be myself, without being afraid. But it's rough. With a background like mine you're always trying to catch up; it's as if you were born two steps behind the next fellow.

[*They type; stop suddenly. They both stare at the audience,* SYLVIA *leaning forward,* PAUL *back in his chair, etc.*]

SYLVIA: My family never had money problems. In that respect we were very fortunate. My father made a good living, while he was alive, that is. He passed away when I was seventeen. You could say he and my mother had a fairly happy marriage. At least we never knew when they were angry with one another, and that's a good thing for children. I have a sister. Charlotte. She's older than I am. She's married now and we don't bother much with each other. But when we were younger you wouldn't believe what went on. Every time we quarrelled, according to my parents she was right; I was always wrong. She got everything she wanted, no matter what, and I had to be content with the left-overs. It was just unbearable. Anyway, my father was sick for a long time before he passed away. He had this ring, it was a beautiful ring, with a large onyx stone in it, and when I was a girl I used to play with it. I'd close one eye and I'd look inside of it and I'd see hundreds and hundreds of beautiful red and blue stars. My father had always promised me that ring; he always said it belonged to me. I thought for certain he'd give it to me before he passed away, but he didn't say anything about it; not a word. Well, afterward, I saw it. You know where I saw it? On my sister's finger. He had given it to her. Now I don't think that's a background that leaves many possibilities for development. I don't forgive my father; definitely not. And I don't forgive my sister. My mother, whom I now support with my hard work, still says I'm wrong.

[*They type; stop suddenly; turn to one another.*]

PAUL: Do you go to the movies?

SYLVIA: Not too often.

PAUL: Me neither.

SYLVIA: Do you like to watch television?

PAUL: I never get the chance. Don't forget I go to school five nights a week. But my wife watches it a lot; that's all she does.

SYLVIA [*surprised*]: I didn't know you were married.

PAUL [*types*]: This machine's full of errors. I'm getting nowhere fast. [*He is about to crumple card.*]

SYLVIA [*rising*]: Let me see that, please. [*Examines card, incommensurate anger.*] Now this could be erased. We don't approve of wasting material when it can be saved. That isn't the policy of this office.

PAUL: Okay. You don't have to be mad. I'll do it.

SYLVIA: I'm not mad. But I am responsible for what goes on in this department. I'm sick and tired of covering up for your mistakes. Everyone must think I'm a piece of rag to be stepped on. First him and now you.

PAUL: Do you mind telling me what you're talking about!

SYLVIA: You know very well what I'm talking about. This is my thanks; this is what I get for trying to be helpful and nice to people. I'm wrong, I know. I'm always wrong. Everything I do is wrong. Well, Mr Cunningham, I've had enough, quite enough, and I won't take any more from you or anyone else. I won't! I won't! [*She flees to the rest-room. Paul slaps the typewriter, goes to telephone, dials.*]

PAUL [*loudly*]: Let me speak to Mr Francis T. Cunningham, please. Who's calling? Paul Cunningham! [*Softly*] Hello, Uncle Frank. It's me again. Paul. How . . . how are you? Everything all right? That's good. Oh, everything's fine with me; still plugging away. I got a new job; yeah, typing, office work; just enough for bread. Uhuh. Uncle, can't you give me a hand? It's too rough for me. I can't hold down a job and go to school five nights a week; it's killing me. I know, I know. But I thought if you could give me a part-time job in your office, or maybe one of your friends, if you spoke to them. . . . Yeah, sure. I understand. It's okay. Yeah. Send my regards.

[PAUL *returns to typewriter.* SYLVIA *enters, exchanges her directory. Her appearance is that of a woman in her thirties.*]

SYLVIA: I'm sorry for losing my temper, Paul. It won't happen again.

PAUL: Forget it. [*He types.*]

SYLVIA: You've become an expert at that machine.

PAUL [*glumly*]: At least I'm an expert at something.

SYLVIA: Is anything the matter?

PAUL: No, but I was just thinking. What am I knocking myself out for? School almost every night, weekends I'm home studying, I can't remember the last time I took a decent vacation. What for? You're young only once; this is the time to enjoy yourself.

SYLVIA [*at typewriter*]: I don't know how true that is. You probably could enjoy yourself a great deal more if you were a lawyer; that's why some sacrifices have to be made now.

PAUL: That's the kind of logic that leads nowhere. By your reasoning all lawyers should be happy men. No, sir; that isn't the way life is. You could be a ditch-digger and be happy if you know how to live. I tell you, I've had it. A fellow in my position has to take advantage of what's offered to him. He's got to be practical and look the facts right in the eye. [*Tapping table*] This here is what's offered to me. This is my chance and from now on I start concentrating on this job. I'll show him I'm on the ball and maybe he'll find something else for me, give me a promotion, a better salary. Why not? An outfit this big always needs men who aren't afraid to work. Listen, I've got two kids at home. I've got to start thinking of them, too.

SYLVIA [*stiffly*]: You have two children?

PAUL: Sure. I don't waste any time. Look, I've got their

pictures here. We took these last summer. [*He shows her photographs inside wallet.*] Well, what do you think?

SYLVIA [*coldly*]: They're beautiful, Paul. What's their names?

PAUL: Frank and Sally. But we call the boy Buddy; he hates it when we call him Frank; funny rascal. They're not bad for a character like me, are they? You know what I'm going to do, Syl? I'm going right in to him and ask him what my chances for advancement are. I might as well get all this settled now. Frankly I can use a little more money, too. The expenses are killing me. If we had a union in this place, we'd get some action. I may do something about that yet. [*He heads for employer's office, turns.*] What . . . what would you say is the best way to approach him?

SYLVIA: I honestly don't know, Paul. He changes from one minute to the next. But if he isn't wearing his glasses, that's a bad sign; I know that much.

PAUL: Glasses . . . I got it. Wish me luck?

SYLVIA: I hope you get something good. [*After* PAUL *exits, she goes to phone, dials.*] Ma? Sylvia. No, I'm all right. Did the lamp come? Well, just make sure when it comes that it isn't damaged; you'll have to sign for it and that means you inspected it. Look at it carefully; if there isn't any damage you can sign, but if there's anything wrong with it, the smallest thing, refuse to sign and tell the man to take it back. Do you understand? I hope so. Did I . . . get any calls? I didn't say I was expecting any, don't put words in my mouth, I merely asked you if I got any. Never mind. It's not important. Did Charlotte call? How is she?

[PAUL *enters. He has the appearance of a man in his thirties.* SYLVIA *carries on the remainder of her call as though talking to a boy-friend.*]

SYLVIA: Oh, stop being silly. I really couldn't. I have something this Saturday. I mean it. [*Laughing*] No, no. Well, perhaps Sunday. Call me at home. All right. Bye.

PAUL [*at typewriter*]: It looks good, real good. He's considering it. He says they may need someone on the sales staff. I'm first on the list.

SYLVIA: That does sound good. What about the raise?

PAUL: I'll have to wait awhile, he said. But I'll get it. He was impressed, especially when I told him I had some legal experience. You should have seen his eyes open up. It's only a question of time, and once I start moving, you watch, it's going to take a pretty fast man to keep up with me.

SYLVIA: You certainly have ambition, Paul.

PAUL [*rises to exchange directory*]: Listen, I don't intend to spend the rest of my life working here or any place else. I'll make my bundle and that's it. There's a world outside that window, a world with a thousand different things to see and do, and I'm going to see and do every last one of them; you watch.

SYLVIA: There's a million different things to do in the world.

PAUL: Lie in the sun . . .

SYLVIA: Dance . . .

PAUL: Travel . . .

SYLVIA: Wear pretty clothes . . .

PAUL: Visit places . . .

SYLVIA: Meet interesting people . . .

PAUL: Mountains. A place with mountains . . .

SYLVIA [*grabs* PAUL'S *lapels, her emotions soaring*]: Oh, Paul, I'm so filled with the desire to live, to experience things, to laugh. . . . Oh, I want to laugh, Paul!

[*Silence.* PAUL *stares dumbly at her, clears his throat. Stiffly they return to their chairs, type energetically.*]

PAUL [*in a moment, calmly*]: When do we have lunch?

SYLVIA: We can have it any time we want. But I usually have it at one. The later you have it the shorter the afternoon is.

PAUL: How about waiting until one-thirty?

SYLVIA: That isn't easy.

PAUL: I know, but then we'd only have a couple of more hours to go. The afternoon would fly. What do you say?

SYLVIA: I'm willing, if you are.

PAUL: It's a deal, then. One-thirty lunch.

[*They shake hands.*]

SYLVIA: One-thirty.

PAUL: Right.

[*They both type.*]

SYLVIA: You know, I'm getting hungry already.

PAUL: So am I. I didn't have any breakfast.

SYLVIA: I had a cup of coffee, that's all.

PAUL: What have you got for lunch?

SYLVIA: A tuna-fish sandwich with tomatoes and mayonnaise, an orange and a piece of layer cake. What did you bring?

PAUL: Two turkey sandwiches and an apple, I think.

SYLVIA: One-thirty.

[*They shake hands.*]

PAUL: That's the deal.

[*They both type.*]

PAUL: We went down to Chinatown last weekend. What a meal we had.

SYLVIA: I'm crazy about Chinese food. I once went with a fellow who knew how to speak Chinese and you should have seen the things he ordered; the most fantastic dishes, with chicken livers and mushrooms and almonds . . .

PAUL: The Chinese people can cook, all right, but when it comes to *real* cooking you can't beat the Italians. There's a place we go to on the West Side; you should taste their veal parmesan or their chicken cacciatore. And they make a spaghetti sauce, you could . . .

SYLVIA [*goes to file cabinet*]: I think I'll eat now.

PAUL [*rising furiously*]: We made a deal, didn't we?

SYLVIA: Don't be childish. If I want to eat now, I'll eat now, and that's all there is to it.

PAUL: You women are all alike. No backbone. No self-discipline. Go ahead and eat, I'm not going to stop you. But I'm sticking to my word.

SYLVIA: I didn't say I was going to eat, Mr Cunningham. I merely said I was thinking of eating; listen before you speak. [*She waves at him blank postcards which she has taken from cabinet.*] And if you want to know something else, I could probably wait longer than you; I could probably go without lunch, which is more than some people can say.

PAUL [*at typewriter*]: Is that so?

SYLVIA [*at typewriter*]: That's so exactly.

PAUL: We'll see, Miss Supervisor.

SYLVIA: You're jealous. It's coming out all over you. I am supervisor . . .

PAUL [*waving his arm*]: Of this whole department. Boy, I'll never forget that as long as I live. [*Mimicking her in a small voice*] 'Believe me, Mr Cunningham, I didn't ask him to be made supervisor. I don't like telling anyone what to do; that's part of my nature. . . .' [*He falls on typewriter in a fit of laughter.*]

SYLVIA: You just keep that up and you won't be working here much longer, I assure you of that, Mr Cunningham.

PAUL: Tell him. Go ahead and tell him. You'd be doing me a favour!

SYLVIA: What? You mean a man with your legal experience, with your plans and ambitions, requires a favour from me?

PAUL: Miss Payton, I loathe you!

SYLVIA: That, Mr Cunningham, would be a gross understatement to describe my feelings for you. You make me sick!

PAUL: Why don't you quit, then?

SYLVIA: Why don't you?

PAUL: I wouldn't give you the satisfaction.

SYLVIA: And I wouldn't give you the satisfaction!
   [*They both type, loudly, rapidly.*]

PAUL [*slaps keys*]: What the hell am I doing? This isn't what I want. No, goddamn it!

SYLVIA [*without looking at him*]: I wonder if the man knows what he wants.

PAUL [*almost ominously*]: You bet I do. And do you know what it is? You know what I'd really like to do? Now, right here in this office? [*Rises, moves around* SYLVIA'S *chair.*] I'd like to rip the clothes right off your back, piece by piece. I'd like to dig my fingers into your flesh and feel your body break and sweat under mine. Do you understand me, Miss Payton?

SYLVIA [*rises; softly*]: Paul.

PAUL: It's been eating me up, ever since I first saw you. I want you, Miss Payton. Now! Now! This minute! Here, on the floor, screaming your lungs out and with your legs kicking up in the air. That's all I've been thinking of at that stupid typewriter; that's all that's been on my mind. [*Pause.*] Now you know.

SYLVIA: And what do you think I've been thinking of? My

body aches with wanting you, Paul. [*Turning, pointing to his typewriter*] How many times have I closed my eyes, just hoping you'd do something instead of sitting there like a stone statue!

[*She falls back into him; he embraces her around the waist, standing behind her.*]

PAUL: Sylvia.

SYLVIA: I'll have to tell my mother, Paul. And you should tell your wife. Oh, I'll be good to the children. I promise you that.

PAUL [*stunned*]: Tell my wife?

SYLVIA: We will get married, won't we?

PAUL: Sylvia, listen . . .

SYLVIA [*turning to face him*]: We will get married, won't we?

PAUL: Aw, the hell with it! I'm going to eat. [*Gets lunch bag, throws coat over arm.*]

SYLVIA [*at typewriter*]: It's my fault, I know; you don't have to tell me.

PAUL: It's nobody's fault. It's . . . the way things are. [*At door*] Can I get you anything?

SYLVIA: I'm not eating.

PAUL: Suit yourself.

[PAUL *exits.* SYLVIA *runs to cabinet, takes out lunch bag; she eats her sandwich ravenously. The door is suddenly thrown open. Quickly* SYLVIA *turns, clutching the sandwich to her chest, hiding it.*]

PAUL: Are you sure you don't want anything?

SYLVIA [*with a mouthful of food*]: Positive.

PAUL: All right.

[PAUL *exits.* SYLVIA *goes to the phone, slowly, lethargically, dials.*]

SYLVIA: Ma? Sylvia. Nothing's wrong. I'm having my lunch now. The sandwich is fine. Did the table come? How is it? Are you sure? Sometimes they get damaged in shipping. Did you look carefully? Well, I hope so. Yes. Did I get any calls? No, I wasn't expecting any; I just asked. [*Pause.*] What did Charlotte say? That's just like her. She could come at least once a week to see how you are. All right, have it your own way. I'm too tired to argue with you. How are the children? That's nice. [*Pause*.] An eighty-five average doesn't mean he's a genius; no, not by any stretch of the imagination. I'm not saying she has stupid children; that isn't what I said, but I can't stand it when you raise them to the sky. I repeat, an eighty-five average is not in the genius class, and if you want proof ask anyone in the educational field. Oh, all right, all right; let's just drop it. I'll see you later. Of course I'm coming home. Where do you think I'd go? Fine. Good-bye. [SYLVIA *throws the remainder of her sandwich into basket, reluctantly sits down at typewriter. As she types and swings the carriage across – for want of something to do – she sings the material she is typing with the lilting intonation of a small girl bouncing a ball on the sidewalk while reciting doggerel.*]

SYLVIA [*typing*]: Mrs Anna Robinson, of 4 East 32nd Street, in the city and state of New York. [*Taking card out, putting new card in; forlornly*] How are you today, Mrs Anna Robinson? It has been so nice talking to you. Who have we here? Oh, it's [*typing*] Mr Arnold Robinson, of 1032 Lexington Avenue, in the city and state of New York. [*Taking card out, putting new card in*] It was so pleasant talking to you, Mr Robinson. Send my regards to the family. Why, if it isn't [*typing*] Mrs Beatrice Robinson, who lives no less on Park Avenue, in the city and state of New York. [*Taking card out, putting new card in*] Must you leave so soon, Mrs Robinson?

[SYLVIA *takes a gumdrop from a bag of candy, continues typing.* PAUL *enters. He is now in his forties. He carries a container of coffee.*]

PAUL [*referring to her candy*]: Up to your old tricks again, Sylvia? You'll never keep your figure that way.

SYLVIA: Don't worry about my figure; just worry about your own.

PAUL [*pulling his stomach in*]: You've got a point there. Here, I brought you some coffee.

SYLVIA: Thanks. [*Gets newspaper.*] How is it outside?

PAUL: A little chilly, but the sun's strong; nice. I took a walk up to the park. You never saw so many characters sitting on the benches and sunning themselves. I sure would like to know how they do it.

SYLVIA: Half of them are probably on relief.

PAUL: We work and they sun themselves.

SYLVIA: You should see the cars some of them have.

PAUL: You don't have to tell me. I know.

SYLVIA: I read in the newspapers that by the year 2000 people will work only three hours a day and have a three-day week.

PAUL: That's not going to help me.

SYLVIA [*at typewriter; opens newspaper*]: We could try to get into a union.

PAUL: Do you know one that isn't crooked?

SYLVIA: How I wish this day was over.

PAUL: It'll feel good getting these shoes off.

SYLVIA: I'll wash my hair and do a little ironing.

PAUL: No date tonight?

SYLVIA: Don't be funny.

PAUL [*at typewriter*]: You know, I was thinking, Syl. Ever since I was a kid I always thought I would like to be independent, to live my own life, without getting involved with responsibilities and families. Inside of me I suppose I always was afraid of that. But, you know, everything I've done in my life has taken me away from what I thought I'd like to be when I was a kid. I got married as soon as I could; I had children right away; I made it so tough for myself I couldn't get through law school. I couldn't live the kind of life I thought I wanted. I've been asking myself lately, what is it I really wanted? You know what the answer to that is, Syl? You know what it has to be? What I got. What I am. Maybe all I really wanted was to be sorry for myself.

SYLVIA: Does anyone know what they want, Paul?

PAUL: Don't you?

SYLVIA: Not any more. I thought I knew, just as you did. But if that's what I wanted, why am I where I am today?

PAUL: It doesn't make sense, does it?

SYLVIA: I swore that at the first opportunity I'd break away from my mother and my sister; I'd have nothing more to do with them and that would be happiness for me. But here I am still living with my mother and every day I ask how my sister is, what she's doing, how her husband is, the children. . . . And I don't give a damn. Not a damn.

PAUL: The things I don't give a damn about . . . Syl, let's look into it. This is important.

SYLVIA: I've always said there's nothing more important than getting to know yourself. When you realize that people can live their whole lives without knowing themselves, without really getting to understand themselves, it . . . it reaches the ridiculous.

PAUL [*rising*]: You're absolutely right.

SYLVIA [*rising*]: Let's see what's behind it all. Let's study it a moment.

PAUL: All right, let's get to it. Why?

SYLVIA: Why?

PAUL: Why do you say that leaving your family would make you happy? If that's all there was to it, you could have left them years ago. No, there's something you're hiding.

SYLVIA: You're not telling the truth. If all you wanted was to feel sorry for yourself, all you'd have to do is sit in a corner and feel sorry for yourself; that's all there is to it. But, no; that isn't it.

PAUL: Then what is it?

SYLVIA: What are you hiding?

[*As one speaks, wagging a finger, the other paces back and forth, nodding without listening, following a separate train of thought.*]

PAUL: The fact remains that you do care what happens to your family, you care a lot, an awful lot; that's why you phone every day, that's why you're always asking about your sister. You have to keep them together; you need them more than they need you because you never developed emotionally enough to forget the past and start a new life for yourself.

SYLVIA: You deliberately put yourself in situations in which you had to fail. Why is it I never heard you say you loved your wife? What was behind your marriage at such an early age? Why didn't you wait until you finished school so that you'd have a fair chance of getting ahead?

PAUL: Simply because you wanted something from them. It had nothing to do with your father's ring; you use that for a smoke screen.

SYLVIA: Now we're coming closer to the truth. You had to rush into marriage, have children and become burdened with impossible responsibilities, the very things you were afraid of; you had to fail because it wasn't that you wanted to feel sorry for yourself, but you wanted other people to feel sorry for you.

PAUL: That's it! They alone could give you what you wanted; no one else, not even a husband; that's why you never got married. Now we're coming closer to it . . .

SYLVIA: So that they would pity and pamper you like a child; you mistook that for love, which was what you really wanted from them, the love which you couldn't get from your parents.

[*They suddenly stand face-to-face.*]

PAUL: There it is! You wanted love!

SYLVIA: You wanted love, of course!

PAUL: Don't you see it now, Syl?

SYLVIA: It's all so clear.

PAUL: When you know something about yourself, then you can start doing something about it.

[*They march back to their typewriters.*]

SYLVIA: This has been one of the most pleasant conversations I've ever had, Paul.

PAUL: I enjoyed it myself. [*Glancing at wrist-watch*] And the afternoon's going pretty fast.

SYLVIA: Thank God for that.

[*They both type.*]

PAUL: You know, thinking about it. I'm sure a lot better off than you are.

SYLVIA: Why's that?

PAUL: Well, I've got a place of my own; I did marry, have children. You could say I fulfilled a pretty important part of my life.

SYLVIA: That's nonsense. Do you think it requires any special ability to get married and have children?

PAUL: All I'm saying is that there are some people who would be awfully glad if they could have gotten married.

SYLVIA: Are you referring to me, Mr Cunningham?

PAUL: I didn't mention any names, did I? But if the shoe fits, wear it, Miss Payton!

SYLVIA [*grimly*]: Don't make me laugh. If I had to make the choice – and I assure you I don't – I would much prefer being single than being forced to continue an unhappy marriage.

PAUL: An unhappy marriage? Where do you get that from? Did you ever hear me say that?

SYLVIA: I can put one and one together, Mr Cunningham. We both know that if you had your way about it you would have left her long ago.

PAUL: Is that right?

SYLVIA: That's exactly right.

PAUL: Well, for your information, Miss Payton, my wife is the finest [*rising*], do you hear me? The finest, the most decent woman I ever had the good fortune to meet.

SYLVIA: Please, Mr Cunningham.

PAUL: And for your further information, I wouldn't trade her for a dozen like you.

SYLVIA: You couldn't possibly. [*The buzzer rings; she fixes her hair, etc.*] Thank God, at last I'll have a moment away from you.

PAUL: I bet you think I don't know what goes on in there?

SYLVIA: What is he raving about now?

PAUL: Go ahead in. I can hear your boy-friend panting behind the door.

SYLVIA: Jealous?

PAUL: Of you?

SYLVIA: It's happened before.

PAUL [*turning away from her, loud undertone*]: You bitch!

SYLVIA [*turning, flaring*]: What did you say? [*No answer.*] You'd better be quiet.

[*She exits.* PAUL *goes to hanger and without unwrapping or removing the whisky bottle from his coat pocket pours a drink into a water cup, swallows it, then fills the cup again. He dials the phone.*]

PAUL: Barbara. Paul. How're the kids? That's good. Oh, pretty much the same. Listen, Barb, I'm . . . I'm sorry about last night. I had a little too much to drink. No, no, don't go excusing it. I just want you to know I didn't mean any of it. I think an awful . . . an awful lot of you, you know that, and I respect you, I always have. It's when I'm drinking, it's the whisky that does the talking. I'm going to stop, I promise you. Barb, you forgive me, don't you? Well, say it; I want to hear you say it; please. [*Pause.*] Thank you. I'll try to get home early and we'll do something, we'll do something different, something . . . different, I promise you. All right. Don't forget. So long.

[*He finishes his drink, crumples cup and slips it into his pocket. Sylvia enters, carrying several sheets of paper, which she places on Paul's typewriter. She is now in her forties.*]

SYLVIA: He wants you to type copies of these. He's waiting for them.

PAUL: What's that?

SYLVIA [*at typewriter*]: You heard me.

PAUL: Well, you hear me now. You can go right in there and tell him to go to hell. I'm not his secretary.

SYLVIA: Why don't you tell him yourself?

PAUL: That's a good idea! [*Moves to employer's office, grabbing papers from typewriter, turns*] That's a damn good idea! [*Exits.*]

SYLVIA [*typing, singsong, as before*]: Mr Thomas Weaver, of 424 Harley Street, in the Bronx, New York. [*Taking card out, putting card in*] I hope that you're having a pleasant day, Mr Thomas Weaver. Now who is this coming along? Oh, it's [*typing*] Miss Tina Lee Weaver, of number 78 Monroe Avenue, in the Bronx, New York. How are you . . .

[PAUL *enters. He shouts at employer's door as he rips papers in half and throws them in the air.*]

PAUL: There, there, that's what I think of you and your job, you old bastard!

SYLVIA: Paul!

PAUL: Why don't you go in and see your boy-friend now? You'll see him hiding behind the desk. If he stayed on his feet like a man I would have punched him right in the nose.

SYLVIA: Did you . . . quit?

PAUL: What the hell do you think I did? Trying to pull that stuff on me. I'm not his secretary and I never was. [*Shouting at employer's door*] Do you hear me, you old bastard! I'm not your secretary and I never was!

SYLVIA [*rising, with concern*]: Please, Paul, be quiet; you're in enough trouble.

PAUL: Trouble? Me? Ha! That's the funniest thing I heard yet. You're looking at a free man, Miss Payton; a free and independent man. Yes, sir. I haven't felt this good in years.

SYLVIA [*following him to coat hanger*]: But what will you do?

PAUL [*removing whisky bottle from coat, throwing wrapper away*]: Start living for one thing; start being myself; start being a man again. You know what it means to be a man, Miss Payton? You don't meet men any more; they're all afraid of losing their jobs, afraid of spending a dollar, afraid of their own shadows. But not this man. No, sir. I don't lick anybody's boots. What are you staring at? This? It's an old custom of mine. Care to join me? No, I didn't think so. [*He drinks from bottle.*]

SYLVIA: Paul, don't; this isn't like you.

PAUL: How do you know what I'm like? How does anybody know? We all live alone, Miss Payton; we all live alone in a cruel and lonely world. [*He drinks.*]

SYLVIA: How true that is.

PAUL: You know what I'm going to do? Yes, sir. The hell with it. I'm dropping everything, leaving everything. The first bus heading west tomorrow, you know who's going to be on it? I am. You bet. [*He raises bottle to mouth.*]

SYLVIA [*tries to take bottle from him*]: Paul, you've had enough of that.

PAUL [*pulls bottle away from her*]: Listen, this is no spur-of-the minute thing with me, and it's not the whisky doing the talking either. I've been thinking of it for a long long time. This city stinks for my money; there's nothing here but a lot of smoke, noise and corruption. I don't know where that bus is going to take me, but I'm not getting off until I find a place where there's plenty of fresh air, lots of room, that's what I want, lots of room, and mountains, mountains as high as you can see. Yes, sir. When I find that place I'm getting off and that's where I'm staying.

SYLVIA: I always dreamt of going somewhere like that, ever since I was a girl; some place away from everyone and everything I know.

PAUL: Do you mean that?

SYLVIA: I'd give anything.

PAUL [*puts bottle on typewriter table*]: Syl.

SYLVIA: Yes, Paul?

PAUL: Listen, we . . . we get along pretty well, don't we?

SYLVIA: We get along extremely well.

PAUL [*standing behind her*]: The times I thought of taking you in my arms and holding you . . .

SYLVIA: Oh, if you only had, Paul.

PAUL: It's not too late, is it?

SYLVIA: No, no, it's not.

PAUL: The two of us, together. [*He holds her about the waist; she clasps his hands.*]

SYLVIA: Oh, Paul, I'm so happy. I'll call my mother. And you call your wife. I don't want there to be any hard feelings. Let's make it as pleasant as possible for everyone.

PAUL [*stunned*]: You want me to call my wife?

SYLVIA: Of course, silly; we're getting married, aren't we?

PAUL: But you don't understand . . .

SYLVIA: We are getting married, aren't we?

PAUL: Aw, what's the use.

SYLVIA: I know; it's my fault; no matter what I do or say it's my fault.

PAUL: No, my fault; it's my fault. I'm no good, Sylvia. I never was. I never had the guts to do anything but feel sorry for myself. I've been a lazy selfish son-of-a-bitch all my life. I never did a damn thing that amounted to a bag of beans. And now. . . . Oh, my God! [*Leaning on typewriter, he sobs loudly.*]

SYLVIA: Paul, stop it; what are you doing? What's wrong?

PAUL: I don't care for myself; it's not for me. My life's over. My wife. . . . [*Shouting*] That bitch can go to hell! But the kids, Sylvia. I love those kids. Now what's going to happen to them? I don't have a job; there's no money put away, nothing. What did I do? What was I trying to prove?

SYLVIA: Why don't you go in and speak to him? Apologize, tell him anything. You're one of the best typists he's ever had; don't forget that.

PAUL: Do you think there's a chance? I can type; no one can

say I can't. That's one thing I can do. Look, Sylvia. Look. [*He stands with his back to the typewriter and with his hands behind him types.*] Check that. Go ahead. You'll find there isn't a single mistake. And this, look at this. [*He stands between both typewriters, spreads his arms out and types on both machines simultaneously.*]

SYLVIA: I know, Paul; you're very good.

PAUL: There. Perfect. Check it. Check it. And this, Sylvia, look at this.

SYLVIA: That's enough, Paul. I believe you. I know you can. . . .

    [*He stands on the chair at his typewriter, removes one shoe, gives it to* SYLVIA, *and types with his stockinged foot, swings carriage across with his large toe, then slumps down in chair.*]

Come down from there. You are good, you're very good.

PAUL: They deserve everything I can give them, Syl. I love those kids. [*He lifts up his foot;* SYLVIA *puts on his shoe.*]

SYLVIA: I know. Now let's get you fixed up so you'll look presentable when you see him. [*Straightens his tie, brushes his jacket, etc.*] Stand still. Stop moving around.

PAUL: He'll never give me another chance, not after what I said to him.

SYLVIA: You just walk in and speak to him. There. Now you look fine. I'll fix things up out here. And we'd better get rid of this bottle. [*She takes it away from him as he raises it to his mouth.*]

PAUL: No more of that for me. I learned my lesson.

SYLVIA: I hope so. Well, go ahead in.

PAUL: Syl, I just want you to know this: if I get my job back, you're going to see some changes. Paul Cunningham has grown up at last.

SYLVIA: Go ahead in.

PAUL: No, not until I thank you for . . . for everything you've done.

SYLVIA: I didn't do a thing.

PAUL: Yes you did; more than I can thank you for. Did you ever think, Syl, what would have happened if the two of us had met before I married Barbara?

SYLVIA [*wistfully*]: Yes, I thought of it, many times.

PAUL [*moving towards her*]: Syl, listen to me . . .

SYLVIA [*raising her hands, moving away from him*]: Not that again. Please. Go in. Go on in.

> [PAUL *exits to employer's office.* SYLVIA *empties whisky bottle in drain of water cooler, then drops bottle into basket; she picks papers from floor; sits at typewriter, puts eye-glasses on, and types.* PAUL *enters. He is now in his fifties.*]

PAUL: It's all right; it's all right. He's taken me back.

SYLVIA: I'm so glad for you.

PAUL: He was darn nice about it, too. He just listened to me and then he said, 'It's understandable, Mr Cunningham. We all have our problems.'

SYLVIA: He can be nice when he wants to.

PAUL: 'We all have our problems.' He's not a stupid man.

SYLVIA: On the contrary, he understands a great many things.

PAUL: You know, we should buy him something; a little gift from the staff, something to show our appreciation. [*Rubbing hands, sits at typewriter*] Well, let's get to it. There's not much left to the day now.

SYLVIA: Yes, soon it'll be over.

> [*They type in silence. Suddenly* PAUL *breaks out in forced laughter.*]

SYLVIA: What's so amusing?

PAUL: Miss Supervisor . . . I'll never forget that as long as I live. 'Believe me, Mr Cunningham, I didn't ask him to be made a supervisor. I don't like telling anyone what to do.'

SYLVIA: We all have our pretensions, Paul.

PAUL [*clearing his throat*]: That's very true.

> [*They type.* SYLVIA *starts to laugh.*]

PAUL: What is it? What . . . what is it? What?

SYLVIA: I was just thinking of a boy I once went with.

PAUL: The Chinese fellow?

SYLVIA: No, no. I don't know any Chinese fellow. This boy was an entertainer. He could make you laugh by just looking at you.

PAUL: Did I ever tell you, Sylvia, that I used to take singing lessons?

SYLVIA: No?

PAUL: I did. When I was eight, nine . . .

SYLVIA [*rises, collects typed cards*]: I didn't know that.

PAUL [*sings*]: Way down upon the Swanee River. . . . Far, far from home. . . .

SYLVIA: You do have a voice.

PAUL [*sings monosyllabically*]: Da, *da*, da, da, da, *da*, da . . .

SYLVIA [*at employer's door*]: *Shh*, not too loudly.

> [SYLVIA *exits, without tidying herself, to employer's office.*
> PAUL *types and sings monosyllabically, using his typewriter as if it were a musical instrument. On the card he has just typed he notices an error, crumples it and slips it into his pocket; he continues singing.* SYLVIA *enters. They are now in their middle sixties, aged, slow-moving, but not grey-wigged, not senile.*]

PAUL [*looking at his watch*]: Sylvia, it's twelve minutes to five.

SYLVIA: We don't generally stop until ten minutes to, Paul.

PAUL: I know. But I thought . . .

SYLVIA: That wouldn't be fair.

PAUL: You're right, as always.

> [*They type.*]

PAUL [*without looking at timepiece*]: Now, Sylvia?

SYLVIA: There's still . . . I would say a minute.

> [*They type.*]

PAUL: Now, Sylvia?

SYLVIA: Yes. . . . Now.

PAUL: Thank God.

SYLVIA: I am tired. A good hot bath and then to bed with me.

> [*Rising he inadvertently brushes a card off the table; he picks it up, reads.*]

PAUL: 'All wool knickers. From factory to you. At a tremendous saving.' Knickers. We've been selling knickers.

SYLVIA [*covering typewriters*]: Come, come, let's put everything away.

PAUL [*going to coat hanger*]: Not many people wear knickers nowadays, do they? Knickers. They're warm, though; and practical, they're very practical.

SYLVIA [*as* PAUL *struggles with his coat*]: Here, let me help you with that. Isn't it too early yet?

PAUL: Just getting ready. [*He helps her put on her coat.*]

SYLVIA: What time is it, Paul? It doesn't feel like five.

PAUL [*looking at wrist-watch*]: Another . . . two minutes.

[*They sit down at typewriters, in their coats, immobile, expressionless, waiting for the two minutes to pass. Then* PAUL *looks at his watch.*]

PAUL [*rising*]: It's time.

SYLVIA [*as they move towards the employer's office*]: I have such a bad recollection. What is this new man's name, Paul?

PAUL: Smith or Stone or . . . I never could remember names.

SYLVIA: We'll give him a friendly good-bye just the same.

[*They stand on the threshold of the office, wave and cry shrilly.*]

PAUL: Good night. Good night in there.

SYLVIA: Have a pleasant evening. Good night.

PAUL: I'll walk you to the subway, Sylvia.

SYLVIA: That would be very nice.

[SYLVIA *stands by the door, buttoning her coat.* PAUL *removes some crumpled cards from his pocket, he looks at them, forlornly, lets them fall from his hands to the floor. He starts towards* SYLVIA *but changes his mind, returns, gets down on his haunches and picks up some crumpled cards; he looks around the office for a place to put them; finding none he slips them back into his pockets and exits with* SYLVIA.]

CURTAIN

ARTHUR MILLER

INCIDENT AT VICHY

For Robert

CHARACTERS

LEBEAU, a painter
BAYARD, an electrician
MARCHAND, a businessman
POLICE GUARD
MONCEAU, an actor
GYPSY
WAITER
BOY
MAJOR
FIRST DETECTIVE
OLD JEW
SECOND DETECTIVE
LEDUC, a doctor
POLICE CAPTAIN
VON BERG, a Prince
PROFESSOR HOFFMAN
FERRAND, a café proprietor
FOUR PRISONERS

First staged by Harold Clurman for the Repertory Theatre of Lincoln Center for the Performing Arts. First performed on 3 December 1964 at the ANTA-Washington Square Theatre, New York City.

CAST

(in order of speaking)

LEBEAU	*Michael Strong*
BAYARD	*Stanley Beck*
MARCHAND	*Paul Mann*
POLICE GUARD	*C. Thomas Blackwell*
MONCEAU	*David J. Stewart*
GYPSY	*Harold Scott*
WAITER	*Jack Waltzer*
BOY	*Ira Lewis*
MAJOR	*Hal Holbrook*
FIRST DETECTIVE	*Alek Primrose*
OLD JEW	*Will Lee*
SECOND DETECTIVE	*James Dukas*
LEDUC	*Joseph Wiseman*
POLICE CAPTAIN	*James Greene*
VON BERG	*David Wayne*
PROFESSOR HOFFMAN	*Clinton Kimbrough*
FERRAND	*Graham Jarvis*
PRISONERS	*Pierre Epstein, Stephen Peters, Tony Lo Bianco, John Vari*

Vichy, France, 1942. A place of detention.

At the right a corridor leads to a turning and an unseen door to the street. Across the back is a structure with two grimy window panes in it – perhaps an office, in any case a private room with a door opening from it at the left.

A long bench stands in front of this room, facing a large empty area whose former use is unclear but which suggests a warehouse, perhaps, an armoury, or part of a railroad station not used by the public. Two small boxes stand apart on either side of the bench.

[*When light begins to rise, six men and a boy of fifteen are dis-covered on the bench in attitudes expressive of their personalities and functions, frozen there like members of a small orchestra at the moment before they begin to play.*

As normal light comes on, their positions flow out of the frieze. It appears that they do not know one another and are sitting like people thrown together in a public place, mutually curious but self-occupied. However, they are anxious and frightened and tend to make themselves small and unobtrusive. Only one, MARCHAND, *a fairly well-dressed businessman, keeps glancing at his watch and bits of paper and calling cards he keeps in his pockets, and seems normally impatient.*

Now, out of hunger and great anxiety, LEBEAU, *a bearded un-kempt man of twenty-five, lets out a dramatized blow of air and leans forward to rest his head on his hands. Others glance at him, then away. He is charged with the energy of fear, and it makes him seem aggressive.*]

LEBEAU: Cup of coffee would be nice. Even a sip.

[*No one responds. He turns to* BAYARD *beside him;* BAYARD

is his age, poorly but cleanly dressed, with a certain muscular austerity in his manner. LEBEAU *speaks in a private undertone.*] You wouldn't have any idea what's going on, would you?

BAYARD [*shaking his head*]: I was walking down the street.

LEBEAU: Me too. Something told me – don't go outside today. So I went out. Weeks go by and I don't open my door. Today I go out. And I had no reason, I wasn't even going anywhere. [*Looks left and right to the others. To* BAYARD] They get picked up the same way?

BAYARD [*shrugs*]: I've only been here a couple of minutes myself – just before they brought you in.

LEBEAU [*looks to the others*]: Does anybody know anything?
    [*They shrug and shake their heads.* LEBEAU *looks at the walls, the room; then he speaks to* BAYARD.]
This isn't a police station, is it?

BAYARD: Doesn't seem so. There's always a desk. It's just some building they're using, I guess.

LEBEAU [*glancing about uneasily, curiously*]: It's painted like a police station, though. There must be an international police paint, they're always the same colour everywhere. Like dead clams, and a little yellow mixed in.
    [*Pause. He glances at the other silent men, and tries to silence himself, like them. But it's impossible, and he speaks to* BAYARD *with a nervous smile.*]
You begin wishing you'd committed a crime, you know? Something definite.

BAYARD [*he is not amused, but not unsympathetic*]: Try to take it easy. It's no good getting excited. We'll find out soon.

LEBEAU: It's just that I haven't eaten since three o'clock yesterday afternoon. Everything gets more vivid when you're hungry – you ever notice that?

BAYARD: I'd give you something, but I forgot my lunch this morning. Matter of fact, I was just turning back to get it when they came up alongside me. Why don't you try to sit back and relax?

LEBEAU: I'm nervous. . . . I mean I'm nervous anyway. [*With a faint, frightened laugh*] I was even nervous before the war.

[*His little smile vanishes. He shifts in his seat. The others wait with subdued anxiety. He notices the good clothes and secure manner of* MARCHAND, *who is at the head of the line, nearest the door. He leans forward to attract him.*]

Excuse me.

[MARCHAND *does not turn to him. He gives a short, sharp, low whistle.* MARCHAND, *already offended, turns slowly to him.*]

Is that the way they picked you up? On the street?

[MARCHAND *turns forward again without answering.*]

Sir?

[MARCHAND *still does not turn back to him.*]

Well, Jesus, pardon me for living.

MARCHAND: It's perfectly obvious they're making a routine identity check.

LEBEAU: Oh.

MARCHAND: With so many strangers pouring into Vichy this past year there're probably a lot of spies and God knows what. It's just a document check, that's all.

LEBEAU [*turns to* BAYARD, *hopefully*]: You think so?

BAYARD [*shrugs; obviously he feels there is something more to it*]: I don't know.

MARCHAND [*to* BAYARD]: Why? There are thousands of people running around with false papers, we all know that. You can't permit such things in wartime.

[*The others glance uneasily at* MARCHAND, *whose sense of security is thereby confined to him alone.*]

Especially now with the Germans starting to take over down here you have to expect things to be more strict, it's inevitable.

[*A pause.* LEBEAU *once again turns to him.*]

LEBEAU: You don't get any . . . special flavour, huh?

MARCHAND: What flavour?

LEBEAU [*glancing at the others*]: Well like . . . some racial . . . implication?

MARCHAND: I don't see anything to fear if your papers are all right. [*He turns front, concluding the conversation.*]

[*Again silence. But* LEBEAU *can't contain his anxiety. He studies* BAYARD'S *profile, then turns to the man on his other side and studies him. Then, turning back to* BAYARD, *he speaks quietly.*]

LEBEAU: Listen, you are . . . Peruvian, aren't you?

BAYARD: What's the matter with you, asking questions like that in here? [*He turns forward.*]

LEBEAU: What am I supposed to do, sit here like a dumb beast?

BAYARD [*laying a calming hand on his knee*]: Friend, it's no good getting hysterical.

LEBEAU: I think we've had it. I think all the Peruvians have had it in Vichy. [*Suppressing a shout*] In 1939 I had an American visa. Before the invasion. I actually had it in my hand . . .

BAYARD: Calm down – this may all be routine.

[*Slight pause. Then . . .*]

LEBEAU: Listen. . . .

[*He leans in and whispers into* BAYARD'S *ear.* BAYARD *glances towards* MARCHAND, *then shrugs to* LEBEAU.]

BAYARD: I don't know, maybe; maybe he's not.

LEBEAU [*desperately attempting familiarity*]: What about you?

BAYARD: Will you stop asking idiotic questions? You're making yourself ridiculous.

LEBEAU: But I am ridiculous, aren't you? In 1939 we were packed for America. Suddenly my mother wouldn't leave the furniture. I'm here because of a brass bed and some fourth-rate crockery. And a stubborn, ignorant woman.

BAYARD: Yes, but it's not all that simple. You should try to think of why things happen. It helps to know the meaning of one's suffering.

LEBEAU: What meaning? If my mother–

BAYARD: It's not your mother. The monopolies got control of Germany. Big business is out to make slaves of everyone, that's why you're here.

LEBEAU: Well I'm not a philosopher, but I know my mother, and that's why I'm here. You're like people who look at my paintings – 'What does this mean, what does that mean?' *Look* at it, don't ask what it means; you're not God, you can't tell what anything means. I'm walking down the street before, a car pulls up beside me, a man gets out and measures my nose, my ears, my mouth, the next thing I'm sitting in a police station – or whatever the hell this is here – and in the middle of Europe, the highest peak of civilization! And you know what it means? After the Romans and the Greeks and the Renaissance, and you know what this means?

BAYARD: You're talking utter confusion.

LEBEAU [*in terror*]: Because I'm utterly confused! [*He suddenly springs up and shouts*] Goddammit, I want some coffee!

[*The* POLICE GUARD *appears at the end of the corridor, a revolver on his hip; he strolls down the corridor and meets* LEBEAU, *who has come halfway up.* LEBEAU *halts, returns to his place on the bench, and sits. The* GUARD *starts to turn to go up the corridor when* MARCHAND *raises his hand.*]

MARCHAND: Excuse me, officer, is there a telephone one can use? I have an appointment at eleven o'clock and it's quite...

[*The* GUARD *simply walks up the corridor, turns the corner, and disappears.* LEBEAU *looks towards* MARCHAND *and shakes his head, laughing silently.*]

LEBEAU [*to Bayard, sotto*]: Isn't it wonderful? The man is probably on his way to work in a German coal mine, and he's worried about breaking an appointment. And people want realistic painting, you see what I mean? [*Slight pause.*] Did they measure your nose? Could you at least tell me that?

BAYARD: No, they just stopped me and asked for my papers. I showed them and they took me in.

MONCEAU [*leaning forward to address* MARCHAND]: I agree with you, sir.

[MARCHAND *turns to him.* MONCEAU *is a bright-eyed, cheerful man of twenty-eight. His clothes were elegant, now frayed. He holds a grey felt hat on his knee, his posture rather elegant.*]

Vichy must be full of counterfeit papers. I think as soon as they start, it shouldn't take long. [*To* LEBEAU] Try to settle down.

LEBEAU [*to* MONCEAU]: Did they measure your nose?

MONCEAU [*disapprovingly*]: I think it'd be best if we all kept quiet.

LEBEAU: What is it, my clothes? How do you know, I might be the greatest painter in France.

MONCEAU: For your sake, I hope you are.

LEBEAU: What a crew! I mean the animosity!
[*Pause.*]

MARCHAND [*leaning forward to see* MONCEAU]: You would think, though, that with the manpower shortage they'd economize on personnel. In the car that stopped me there was a driver, two French detectives, and a German official of some kind. They could easily have put a notice in the paper – everyone would have come here to present his documents. This way it's a whole morning wasted. Aside from the embarrassment.

LEBEAU: I'm not embarrassed. I'm scared to death. [*To* BAYARD] You embarrassed?

BAYARD: Look, if you can't be serious just leave me alone.
[*Pause.* LEBEAU *leans forward to see the man sitting on the far side of* MARCHAND. *He points.*]

LEBEAU: Gypsy?

GYPSY [*drawing closer a copper pot at his feet*]: Gypsy.

LEBEAU [*to* MONCEAU]: Gypsies never have papers. Why'd they bother him?

MONCEAU: In his case it might be some other reason. He probably stole that pot.

GYPSY: No. On the sidewalk. [*He raises the pot from between his feet.*] I fix, make nice. I sit down to fix. Come police. Pfft!

MARCHAND: But of course they'll tell you anything. . . . [*To* GYPSY, *laughing familiarly*] Right?
[GYPSY *laughs and turns away to his own gloom.*]

LEBEAU: That's a hell of a thing to say to him. I mean, would you say that to a man with pressed pants?

MARCHAND: They don't mind. In fact, they're proud of stealing. [*To* GYPSY] Aren't you?
[GYPSY *glances at him, shrugs.*]
I've got a place in the country where they come every summer. I like them, personally – especially the music. [*With a broad grin he sings towards the* GYPSY *and laughs.*] We often listen to them around their campfires. But they'll steal the eyes out of your head. [*To* GYPSY] Right?
[GYPSY *shrugs and kisses the air contemptuously.* MARCHAND *laughs with brutal familiarity.*]

LEBEAU: Why shouldn't he steal? How'd you get *your* money?

MARCHAND: I happen to be in business.

LEBEAU: So what have you got against stealing?

BAYARD: Are you trying to provoke somebody? Is that it?

LEBEAU: Another businessman.

BAYARD: I happen to be an electrician. But a certain amount of solidarity wouldn't hurt right now.

LEBEAU: How about some solidarity with Gypsies? Just because they don't work nine to five?

WAITER [*a small man, middle-aged, still wearing his apron*]: I know this one. I've made him go away a hundred times. He and his wife stand outside the café with a baby, and they beg. It's not even their baby.

LEBEAU: So what? They've still got a little imagination.

WAITER: Yes, but they keep whining to the customers through the shrubbery. People don't like it.

LEBEAU: You know – you all remind me of my father. Always worshipped the hard-working Germans. And now you hear it all over France – we have to learn how to work like the Germans. Good God, don't you ever read history? Whenever a people starts to work hard, watch out, they're going to kill somebody.

BAYARD: That depends on how production is organized. If it's for private profit, yes, but–

LEBEAU: What are you talking about, when did the Russians start getting dangerous? When they learned how to work. Look at the Germans – for a thousand years peaceful, disorganized people – they start working and they're on everybody's back. Nobody's afraid of the Africans, are they? Because they don't work. Read the Bible – work is a curse, you're not supposed to worship work.

MARCHAND: And how do you propose to produce anything?

LEBEAU: Well that's the problem.

[MARCHAND *and* BAYARD *laugh.*]

What are you laughing at? *That is the problem!* Yes! To work without making work a god! What kind of crew is this?

[*The office door opens and the* MAJOR *comes out. He is twenty-eight, a wan but well-built man; there is something ill about him. He walks with a slight limp, passing the line of men as he goes towards the corridor.*]

WAITER: Good morning, Major.

MAJOR [*startled, nods to the* WAITER]: Oh. Good morning. [*He continues up the corridor, where he summons the* GUARD *around the corner – the* GUARD *appears and they talk unheard.*]

MARCHARD [*sotto*]: You know him?

WAITER [*proudly*]: I serve him breakfast every morning. Tell you the truth, he's really not a bad fellow. Regular army, see, not one of these S.S. bums. Got wounded somewhere, so they stuck him back here. Only came about a month ago, but he and I–

[*The* MAJOR *comes back down the corridor. The* GUARD *returns to his post out of sight at the corridor's end. As the* MAJOR *passes* MARCHAND . . .]

MARCHAND [*leaping up and going to the* MAJOR]: Excuse me, sir.

[*The* MAJOR *slowly turns his face to* MARCHAND. MARCHAND *affects to laugh deferentially.*]

I hate to trouble you, but I would be much obliged if I could use a telephone for one minute. In fact, it's business connected to the food supply. I am the manager of . . .

[*He starts to take out a business card, but the* MAJOR *has turned away and walks to the door. But there he stops and turns back.*]

MAJOR: I'm not in charge of this procedure. You will have to wait for the Captain of Police. [*He goes into the office.*]

MARCHAND: I beg your pardon.

[*The door has been closed on his line. He goes back to his place and sits, glaring at the* WAITER.]

WAITER: He's not a really bad fellow.

[*They all look at him, eager for some clue.*]

He even comes at night sometimes, plays a beautiful piano. Gives himself French lessons out of a book. Always has a few nice words to say, too.

LEBEAU: Does he know that you're a . . . Peruvian?

BAYARD [*instantly*]: Don't discuss that here, for God's sake! What's the matter with you?

LEBEAU: Can't I find out what's going on? If it's a general identity check it's one thing, but if–

[*From the end of the corridor enter* FIRST DETECTIVE *with the* OLD JEW, *a man in his seventies, bearded, carrying a large sackcloth bundle; then the* SECOND DETECTIVE, *holding the arm of* LEDUC; *then the* POLICE CAPTAIN, *uniformed, with* VON BERG; *and finally the* PROFESSOR *in civilian clothes.*

The FIRST DETECTIVE *directs the* OLD JEW *to sit, and he does, beside the* GYPSY. *The* SECOND DETECTIVE *directs* VON BERG *to sit beside the* OLD JEW. *Only now does the* SECOND DETECTIVE *release his hold on* LEDUC *and indicate that he is to sit beside* VON BERG.]

SECOND DETECTIVE [*to* LEDUC]: Don't you give me any more trouble now.

[*The door opens and the* MAJOR *enters. Instantly* LEDUC *is on his feet, approaching the* MAJOR.]

LEDUC: Sir, I must ask the reason for this. I am a combat officer, captain in the French Army. There is no authority to arrest me in French territory. The Occupation has not revoked French law in southern France.

[*The* SECOND DETECTIVE, *infuriated, throws* LEDUC *back into his seat. He returns to the* PROFESSOR.]

SECOND DETECTIVE [*to* MAJOR, *of* LEDUC]: Speech-maker.

PROFESSOR [*doubtfully*]: You think you two can carry on now?

SECOND DETECTIVE: We got the idea, Professor. [*To the* MAJOR] There's certain neighbourhoods they head for when they run away from Paris or wherever they come from. I can get you as many as you can handle.

FIRST DETECTIVE: It's a question of knowing the neighbourhoods, you see. In my opinion, you've got at least a couple thousand in Vichy on false papers.

PROFESSOR: You go ahead, then.

[*As the* SECOND DETECTIVE *turns to go with the* FIRST DETECTIVE, *the* POLICE CAPTAIN *calls him.*]

CAPTAIN: Saint-Père.

SECOND DETECTIVE: Yes, sir.

[*The* CAPTAIN *walks downstage with the* DETECTIVE.]

CAPTAIN: Try to avoid taking anybody out of a crowd. Just cruise around the way we did before, and take them one at a time. There are all kinds of rumours. We don't want to alarm people.

SECOND DETECTIVE: Right, sir.

    [*The* CAPTAIN *gestures, and both* DETECTIVES *leave up the corridor.*]

CAPTAIN: I am just about to order coffee. Will you gentlemen have some?

PROFESSOR: Please.

WAITER [*timidly*]: And a croissant for the Major.

    [*The* MAJOR *glances quickly at the* WAITER *and barely smiles. The* CAPTAIN, *who has thrown a mystified look at the* WAITER, *goes into the office.*]

MARCHAND [*to the* PROFESSOR]: I believe I am first, sir.

PROFESSOR: Yes, this way. [*He goes into the office, followed by the eager* MARCHAND.]

MARCHAND [*going in*]: Thank you. I'm in a dreadful hurry. . . . I was on my way to the Ministry of Supply, in fact. . . .

    [*His voice is lost within. As the* MAJOR *reaches the door,* LEDUC, *who has been in a fever of calculation, calls to him.*]

LEDUC: Amiens.

MAJOR [*he halts at the door, turns to* LEDUC, *who is at the far end of the line*]: What about Amiens?

LEDUC [*suppressing his nervousness*]: June ninth, 'forty. I was in the Sixteenth Artillery, facing you. I recognize your insignia, which of course I could hardly forget.

MAJOR: That was a bad day for you fellows.

LEDUC: Yes. And evidently for you.

MAJOR [*glances down at his leg*]: Can't complain.

    [*The* MAJOR *goes into the office, shuts the door. A pause.*]

LEDUC [*to all*]: What's this all about?

WAITER [*to all*]: I told you he wasn't a bad guy. You'll see.

MONCEAU [*to* LEDUC]: It seems they're checking on identification papers.

    [LEDUC *receives the news, and obviously grows cautious and quietly alarmed. He examines their faces.*]

LEDUC: What's the procedure?

MONCEAU: They've just started – that businessman was the first.

LEBEAU [*to* LEDUC *and* VON BERG]: They measure your noses?

LEDUC [*sharply alarmed*]: Measure noses?

LEBEAU [*putting thumb and forefinger against the bridge and tip of his nose*]: Ya, they measured my nose, right on the street. I tell you what I think. . . . [*To* BAYARD] With your permission.

BAYARD: I don't mind you talking as long as you're serious.

LEBEAU: I think it's to carry stones. It just occurred to me – last Monday a girl I know came up from Marseille – the road is full of detours. They probably need labour. She said there was a crowd of people just carrying stones. Lot of them Jews she thought: hundreds.

LEDUC: I never heard of forced labour in the Vichy Zone. Is that going on here?

BAYARD: Where do you come from?

LEDUC [*slight pause – he decides whether to reveal*]: I live in the country. I don't get into town very often. There's been no forced-labour decree, has there?

BAYARD [*to all*]: Now, listen. [*Everyone turns to his straight-forward, certain tone.*] I'm going to tell you something, but I don't want anybody quoting me. Is that understood?

[*They nod. He glances at the door. He turns to* LEBEAU.]
You hear what I said?

LEBEAU: Don't make me out some kind of an idiot. Christ's sake, I know it's serious!

BAYARD [*to the others*]: I work in the railroad yards. A thirty-car freight train pulled in yesterday. The engineer is Polish, so I couldn't talk to him, but one of the switchmen says he heard people inside.

LEDUC: Inside the cars?

BAYARD: Yes. It came from Toulouse. I heard there's been a quiet round-up of Jews in Toulouse the last couple of weeks. And what's a Polish engineer doing on a train in southern France? You understand?

LEDUC: Concentration camp?

MONCEAU: Why? A lot of people have been volunteering for work in Germany. That's no secret. They're doubling the ration for anybody who goes.

BAYARD [*quietly*]: The cars are locked on the outside. [*Slight pause.*] And they stink. You can smell the stench a hundred

yards away. Babies are crying inside. You can hear them.
And women. They don't lock volunteers in that way. I
never heard of it.

[*A long pause.*]

LEDUC: But I've never heard of them applying the Racial
Laws down here. It's still French territory, regardless of the
Occupation – they've made a big point of that.

[*Pause.*]

BAYARD: The Gypsy bothers me.

LEBEAU: Why?

BAYARD: They're in the same category of the Racial Laws.
Inferior.

[LEDUC *and* LEBEAU *slowly turn to look at the* GYPSY.]

LEBEAU [*turning back quickly to* BAYARD]: Unless he really stole
that pot.

BAYARD: Well, yes, if he stole the pot then of course he–

LEBEAU [*quickly, to the* GYPSY]: Hey, listen. [*He gives a soft,
sharp whistle. The* GYPSY *turns to him.*] You steal that pot?

[*The* GYPSY'S *face is inscrutable.* LEBEAU *is embarrassed to
press this, and more desperate.*]

You did, didn't you?

GYPSY: No steal, no.

LEBEAU: Look, I've got nothing against stealing. [*Indicating
the others*] I'm not one of these types. I've slept in parked
cars, under bridges – I mean, to me all property is theft
anyway so I've got no prejudice against you.

GYPSY: No steal.

LEBEAU: Look . . . I mean you're a Gypsy, so how else can you
live, right?

WAITER: He steals everything.

LEBEAU [*to* BAYARD]: You hear? He's probably in for stealing,
that's all.

VON BERG: Excuse me. . . .

[*They turn to him.*]

Have you all been arrested for being Jewish?

[*They are silent, suspicious and surprised.*]

I'm terribly sorry. I had no idea.

BAYARD: I said nothing about being Jewish. As far as I know,
nobody here is Jewish.

VON BERG: I'm terribly sorry.

> [*Silence. The moment lengthens. In his embarrassment he laughs nervously.*]

It's only that I . . . I was buying a newspaper and this gentleman came out of a car and told me I must have my documents checked. I . . . I had no idea.

> [*Silence. Hope is rising in them.*]

LEBEAU [*to* BAYARD]: So what'd they grab *him* for?

BAYARD [*looks at* VON BERG *for a moment, then addresses all*]: I don't understand it, but take my advice. If anything like that happens and you find yourself on that train . . . there are four bolts halfway up the doors on the inside. Try to pick up a nail or a screwdriver, even a sharp stone – you can chisel the wood out around those bolts and the doors will open. I warn you, don't believe anything they tell you – I heard they're working Jews to death in the Polish camps.

MONCEAU: I happen to have a cousin; they sent him to Auschwitz; that's in Poland, you know. I have several letters from him saying he's fine. They've even taught him bricklaying.

BAYARD: Look, friend, I'm telling you what I heard from people who know. [*Hesitates.*] People who make it their business to know, you understand? Don't listen to any stories about resettlement, or that they're going to teach you a trade or something. If you're on that train get out before it gets where it's going.

> [*Pause.*]

LEDUC: I've heard the same thing.

> [*They turn to him and he turns to* BAYARD.]

How would one find tools, you have any idea?

MONCEAU: This is so typical! We're in the French Zone, nobody has said one word to us, and we're already on a train for a concentration camp where we'll be dead in a year.

LEDUC: But if the engineer is a Pole . . .

MONCEAU: So he's a Pole, what does that prove?

BAYARD: All I'm saying is that if you have some kind of tool . . .

LEDUC: I think what this man says should be taken seriously.

MONCEAU: In my opinion you're hysterical. After all, they were picking up Jews in Germany for years before the war, they've been doing it in Paris since they came in – are you telling me all those people are dead? Is that really conceivable to you? War is war, but you still have to keep a certain sense of proportion. I mean Germans are still *people*.

LEDUC: I don't speak this way because they're Germans.

BAYARD: It's that they're Fascists.

LEDUC: Excuse me, no. It's exactly because they are people that I speak this way.

BAYARD: I don't agree with *that*.

MONCEAU [*looks at* LEDUC *for an instant*]: You must have had a peculiar life, is all I can say. I happen to have played in Germany; I know the German people.

LEDUC: I studied in Germany for five years, and in Austria and I–

VON BERG [*happily*]: In Austria! Where?

LEDUC [*again he hesitates, then reveals*]: The Psychoanalytic Institute in Vienna.

VON BERG: Imagine!

MONCEAU: You're a psychiatrist. [*To the others*] No wonder he's so pessimistic!

VON BERG: Where did you live? I am Viennese.

LEDUC: Excuse me, but perhaps it would be wiser not to speak in . . . detail.

VON BERG [*glancing about as though he had committed a gaffe*]: I'm terribly sorry . . . yes, of course. [*Slight pause.*] I was only curious if you knew Baron Kessler. He was very interested in the medical school.

LEDUC [*with an odd coolness*]: No, I was never in that circle.

VON BERG: Oh, but he is extremely democratic. He . . . [*shyly*] he is my cousin, you see. . . .

LEBEAU: You're a nobleman?

VON BERG: Yes.

LEDUC: What is your name?

VON BERG: Wilhelm Johann Von Berg.

MONCEAU [*astonished, impressed*]: The prince?

VON BERG: Yes . . . forgive me, have we met?

MONCEAU [*excited by the honour*]: Oh, no. But naturally I've heard your name. I believe it's one of the oldest houses in Austria.

VON BERG: Oh, that's of no importance any more.

LEBEAU [*turning to* BAYARD – *bursting with hope*]: Now, what the hell would they want with an Austrian prince?

[BAYARD *looks at* VON BERG, *mystified.*]

I mean . . . [*Turning back to* VON BERG] You're Catholic, right?

VON BERG: Yes.

LEDUC: But is your title on your papers?

VON BERG: Oh, yes, my passport.

[*Pause. They sit silent, on the edge of hope, but bewildered.*]

BAYARD: Were you . . . political or something?

VON BERG: No, no, I never had any interest in that direction. [*Slight pause.*] Of course, there is this resentment toward the nobility. That might explain it.

LEDUC: In the Nazis? Resentment?

VON BERG [*surprised*]: Yes, certainly.

LEDUC [*with no evident viewpoint but with a neutral but pressing interest in drawing the nobleman out*]: Really. I've never been aware of that.

VON BERG: Oh, I assure you.

LEDUC: But on what ground?

VON BERG [*laughs, embarrassed to have to even suggest he is offended*]: You're not asking that seriously.

LEDUC: Don't be offended. I'm simply ignorant of that situation. I suppose I have taken for granted that the aristocracy is . . . always behind a reactionary régime.

VON BERG: Oh, there are some, certainly. But for the most part they never took responsibility, in any case.

LEDUC: That interests me. So you still take seriously the . . . the title and . . .

VON BERG: It is not a 'title'; it is my name, my family. Just as you have a name, and a family. And you are not inclined to dishonour them, I presume.

LEDUC: I see. And by responsibility, you mean, I suppose, that–

VON BERG: Oh, I don't know; whatever that means. [*He glances at his watch.*]

[*Pause.*]

LEDUC: Please forgive me, I didn't mean to pry into your

affairs. [*Pause.*] I'd never thought about it, but it's obvious now – they *would* want to destroy whatever power you have.

VON BERG: Oh, no, I have no power. And if I did it would be a day's work for them to destroy it. That's not the issue. [*Pause.*]

LEDUC [*fascinated – he is drawn to some truth in* VON BERG]: What is it, then? Believe me, I'm not being critical. Quite the contrary . . .

VON BERG: But these are obvious answers! [*He laughs.*] I have a certain . . . standing. My name is a thousand years old, and they know the danger if someone like me is perhaps . . . not vulgar enough.

LEDUC: And by vulgar you mean . . .

VON BERG: Well, don't you think Nazism . . . whatever else it may be . . . is an outburst of vulgarity? An ocean of vulgarity?

BAYARD: I'm afraid it's a lot more than that, my friend.

VON BERG [*politely, to* BAYARD]: I am sure it is, yes.

BAYARD: You make it sound like they have bad table manners, that's all.

VON BERG: They certainly do, yes. Nothing angers them more than a sign of any . . . refinement. It is decadent, you see.

BAYARD: What kind of statement is that? You mean you left Austria because of their table manners?

VON BERG: Table manners, yes; and their adoration of dreadful art; and grocery clerks in uniform telling the orchestra what music it may not play. Vulgarity can be enough to send a man out of his country, yes, I think so.

BAYARD: In other words, if they had good taste in art, and elegant table manners, and let the orchestra play whatever it liked, they'd be all right with you.

VON BERG: But how would that be possible? Can people with respect for art go about hounding Jews? Making a prison of Europe, pushing themselves forward as a race of policemen and brutes? Is that possible for artistic people?

MONCEAU: I'd like to agree with you, Prince von Berg, but I have to say that the German audiences – I've played there – no audience is as sensitive to the smallest nuance of a performance; they sit in the theatre with respect, like in a church. And nobody listens to music like a German. Don't you think so? It's a passion with them.

[*Pause.*]

VON BERG [*appalled at the truth*]: I'm afraid that is true, yes. [*Pause.*] I don't know what to say. [*He is depressed, deeply at a loss.*]

LEDUC: Perhaps it isn't those people who are doing this.

VON BERG: I'm afraid I know many cultivated people who ... did become Nazis. Yes, they did. Art is perhaps no defence against this. It's curious how one takes certain ideas for granted. Until this moment I had thought of art as a ... [*To* BAYARD] You may be right – I don't understand very much about it. Actually, I'm essentially a musician – in an amateur way, of course, and politics has never ...

[*The office door opens and* MARCHAND *appears, backing out, talking to someone within. He is putting a leather document-wallet into his breast pocket, while with the other hand he holds a white pass.*]

MARCHAND: That's perfectly all right, I understand perfectly. Good day, gentlemen. [*Holding up the pass to them*] I show the pass at the door? Thank you. [*Shutting the door, he turns and hurries past the line of prisoners, and, as he passes the* BOY ...]

BOY: What'd they ask you, sir?

[MARCHAND *turns up the corridor without glancing at the* BOY, *and as he approaches the end the* GUARD, *hearing him, appears there. He hands the pass to the* GUARD *and goes out. The* GUARD *moves around the turning of the corridor and disappears.*]

LEBEAU [*half mystified, half hopeful*]: I could have sworn he was a Jew! [*To* BAYARD] Didn't you think so?

[*Slight pause.*]

BAYARD [*clearly he did think so*]: You have papers, don't you?

LEBEAU: Oh sure, I have good papers. [*He takes rumpled documents out of his pants pocket.*]

BAYARD: Well, just insist they're valid. Maybe that's what he did.

LEBEAU: I wish you'd take a look at them, will you?

BAYARD: I'm no expert.

LEBEAU: I'd like your opinion, though. You seem to know what's going on. How they look to you?

[BAYARD *quickly hides the papers as the office door opens. The* PROFESSOR *appears and indicates the* GYPSY.]

PROFESSOR: Next. You. Come with me.

[*The* GYPSY *gets up and starts towards him. The* PROFESSOR *indicates the pot in the* GYPSY'S *hand.*]

You can leave that.

[*The* GYPSY *hesitates, glances at the pot.*]

I said leave it there.

[*The* GYPSY *puts the pot down on the bench unwillingly.*]

GYPSY: Fix. No steal.

PROFESSOR: Go in.

GYPSY [*indicating the pot, warning the others*]: That's mine.

[*The* GYPSY *goes into the office. The* PROFESSOR *follows him in and shuts the door.* BAYARD *takes the pot, bends the handle off, puts it in his pocket, and sets the pot back where it was.*]

LEBEAU [*turning back to* BAYARD, *indicating his papers*]: What do you think?

BAYARD [*holds a paper up to the light, turns it over, gives it back to* LEBEAU]: Look good far as I can tell.

MONCEAU: That man did seem Jewish to me. Didn't he to you, Doctor?

LEDUC: I have no idea. Jews are not a race, you know. They can look like anybody.

LEBEAU [*with the joy of near-certainty*]: He just probably had good papers. Because I know people have papers, I mean all you have to do is look at them and you know they're phoney. But I mean if you have good papers, right?

[MONCEAU *has meanwhile taken out his papers and is examining them. The* BOY *does the same with his.* LEBEAU *turns to* LEDUC.]

That's true, though. My father looks like an Englishman. The trouble is I took after my mother.

BOY [*to* BAYARD, *offering his papers*]: Could you look at mine?

BAYARD: I'm no expert, kid. Anyway, don't sit there looking at them like that.

[MONCEAU *puts his away, as the* BOY *does. A pause. They wait.*]

MONCEAU: I think it's a question of one's credibility – that man just now did carry himself with a certain confidence. . . .

[*The* OLD JEW *begins to pitch forward on to the floor.* VON BERG *catches him and with the* BOY *helps him back on to the seat.*]

LEBEAU [*with heightened nervousness*]: Christ, you'd think they'd shave off their beards. I mean, to walk around with a beard like that in a country like this!

[MONCEAU *looks at his beard, and* LEBEAU *touches it.*]

Well, I just don't waste time shaving, but . . .

VON BERG [*to the* OLD JEW]: Are you all right, sir?

[LEDUC *bends over* VON BERG'S *lap and feels the* OLD JEW'S *pulse. He lets his hand go, and looks towards* LEBEAU.]

LEDUC: Were you serious? They actually measured your nose?

LEBEAU: With his fingers. That civilian. They called him 'professor'. [*Pause. Then, to* BAYARD] I think you're right; it's all a question of your papers. That businessman certainly looked Jewish. . . .

MONCEAU: I'm not so sure now.

LEBEAU [*angrily*]: A minute ago you were sure, now suddenly . . .!

MONCEAU: Well, even if he wasn't – it only means it really is a general check-up. On the whole population.

LEBEAU: Hey, that's right too! [*Slight pause.*] Actually, I'm often taken for a gentile myself. Not that I give a damn but most of the time, I . . . [*To* VON BERG] How about you, they measure your nose?

VON BERG: No, they told me to get into the car, that was all.

LEBEAU: Because actually yours looks bigger than mine.

BAYARD: Will you cut that out! Just cut it out, will you?

LEBEAU: Can't I try to find out what I'm in for?

BAYARD: Did you ever think of anything beside yourself? Just because you're an artist? You people demoralize everybody.

LEBEAU [*with unconcealed terror*]: What the hell am I supposed to think of? Who're you thinking of?

[*The office door opens. The* POLICE CAPTAIN *appears, and gestures towards* BAYARD.]

CAPTAIN: Come inside here.

[BAYARD, *trying hard to keep his knees from shaking, stands.*
FERRAND, *a café proprietor, comes hurrying down the corridor
with a tray of coffee things covered with a large napkin. He has
an apron on.*]

Ah, at last!

FERRAND: Sorry, Captain, but for you I had to make some
fresh.

CAPTAIN [*as he goes into the office behind* FERRAND]: Put it on
my desk.

[*The door is closed.* BAYARD *sits, wipes his face. Pause.*]

MONCEAU [*to* BAYARD, *quietly*]: Would you mind if I made a
suggestion?

[BAYARD *turns to him, already defensive.*]

You looked terribly uncertain of yourself when you stood
up just now.

BAYARD [*taking offence*]: Me uncertain? You've got the wrong
man.

MONCEAU: Please, I'm not criticizing you.

BAYARD: Naturally I'm a little nervous, facing a room full of
Fascists like this.

MONCEAU: But that's why one must seem especially self-
confident. I'm quite sure that's what got that businessman
through so quickly. I've had similar experiences on trains,
and even in Paris when they stopped me several times. The
important thing is not to look like a victim. Or even to feel
like one. They can be very stupid, but they do have a sense
for victims; they know when someone has nothing to hide.

LEDUC: But how does one avoid feeling like a victim?

MONCEAU: One must create one's own reality in this world.
I'm an actor, we do this all the time. The audience, you
know, is very sadistic; it looks for your first sign of weak-
ness. So you must try to think of something that makes you
feel self-assured; anything at all. Like the day, perhaps, when
your father gave you a compliment, or a teacher was amazed
at your cleverness. . . . Any thought [*to* BAYARD] that makes
you feel . . . valuable. After all, you are trying to create an
illusion; to make them believe you are who your papers say
you are.

LEDUC: That's true, we must not play the part they have

written for us. That's very wise. You must have great courage.

MONCEAU: I'm afraid not. But I have talent instead. [*To BAYARD*] One must show them the face of a man who is right, not a man who is suspect and wrong. They sense the difference.

BAYARD: My friend, you're in a bad way if you have to put on an act to feel your rightness. The bourgeoisie sold France; they let in the Nazis to destroy the French working class. Remember the causes of this war and you've got *real* confidence.

LEDUC: Excepting that the causes of this war keep changing so often.

BAYARD: Not if you understand the economic and political forces.

LEDUC: Still, when Germany attacked us the Communists refused to support France. They pronounced it an imperialist war. Until the Nazis turned against Russia; then in one afternoon it all changed into a sacred battle against tyranny. What confidence can one feel from an understanding that turns upside down in an afternoon?

BAYARD: My friend, without the Red Army standing up to them right now you could forget France for a thousand years!

LEDUC: I agree. But that does not require an understanding of political and economic forces – it is simply faith in the Red Army.

BAYARD: It is faith in the future; and the future is Socialist. And that is what *I* take in there with *me*. [*To the others*] I warn you – I've had experience with these types. You'd better ram a viewpoint up your spine or you'll break in half.

LEDUC: I understand. You mean it's important not to feel alone, is that it?

BAYARD: None of us is alone. We're members of history. Some of us don't know it, but you'd better learn it for your own preservation.

LEDUC: That we are . . . symbols.

BAYARD [*uncertain whether to agree*]: Yes. Why not? Symbols, yes.

LEDUC: And you feel that helps you. Believe me, I am genuinely interested.

BAYARD: It helps me because it's the truth. What am I to them personally? Do they know me? You react personally to this, they'll turn you into an idiot. You can't make sense of this on a personal basis.

LEDUC: I agree. [*Personally*] But the difficulty is – what can one be if not oneself? For example, the thought of torture or something of that sort . . .

BAYARD [*struggling to live his conviction*]: Well, it frightens me – of course. But they can't torture the future; it's out of their hands. Man was not made to be the slave of Big Business. Whatever they do, something inside me is laughing. Because they can't win. Impossible. [*He has stiffened himself against his rising fear.*]

LEDUC: So that in a sense . . . you aren't here. You personally.

BAYARD: In a sense. Why, what's wrong with that?

LEDUC: Nothing; it may be the best way to hold on to oneself. It's only that ordinarily one tries to experience life, to be in spirit where one's body is. For some of us it's difficult to shift gears and go into reverse. But that's not a problem for you.

BAYARD [*solicitously*]: You think a man can ever be himself in this society? When millions go hungry and a few live like kings, and whole races are slaves to the stock market – how can you be yourself in such a world? I put in ten hours a day for a few francs. I see people who never bend their backs and they own the planet. . . . How can my spirit be where my body is? I'd have to be an ape.

VON BERG: Then where is your spirit?

BAYARD: In the future. In the day when the working class is master of the world. *That's* my confidence. . . . [*To* MON-CEAU] Not some borrowed personality.

VON BERG [*wide-eyed, genuinely asking*]: But don't you think . . . excuse me. Are not most Nazis . . . of the working class?

BAYARD: Well, naturally, with enough propaganda you can confuse anybody.

VON BERG: I see. [*Slight pause.*] But in that case, how can one have such confidence in them?

BAYARD: Who do you have confidence in, the aristocracy?

VON BERG: Very little. But in certain aristocrats, yes. And in certain common people.

BAYARD: Are you telling me that history is a question of 'certain people'? Are we sitting here because we are 'certain people'? Is any of us an individual to them? Class interest makes history, not individuals.

VON BERG: Yes. That seems to be the trouble.

BAYARD: Facts are not trouble. A human being has to glory in the facts.

VON BERG [*with a deep, anxious out-reaching to* BAYARD]: But the facts. . . . Dear sir, what if the facts are dreadful? And will always be dreadful?

BAYARD: So is childbirth, so is . . .

VON BERG: But a child comes of it. What if nothing comes of the facts but endless, endless disaster? Believe me, I am happy to meet a man who is not cynical; any faith is precious these days. But to give your faith to a . . . a class of people is impossible, simply impossible – ninety-nine per cent of the Nazis are ordinary working-class people!

BAYARD: I concede it *is* possible to propagandize . . .

VON BERG [*with an untoward anxiety, as though the settlement of this issue is intimate with him*]: But what can *not* be propagandized? Isn't that the . . . the only point? A few individuals. Don't you think so?

BAYARD: You're an intelligent man, Prince. Are you seriously telling me that five, ten, a thousand, ten thousand decent people of integrity are all that stand between us and the end of everything? You mean this whole world is going to hang on that thread?

VON BERG [*struck*]: I'm afraid it does sound impossible.

BAYARD: If I thought that, I wouldn't have the strength to walk through that door, I wouldn't know how to put one foot in front of the other.

VON BERG [*slight pause*]: Yes. I hadn't really considered it that way. But . . . you really think the working class will . . .

BAYARD: They will destroy Fascism because it is against their interest.

VON BERG [*nods*]: But in that case, isn't it even more of a mystery?

BAYARD: I see no mystery.

VON BERG: But they adore Hitler.

BAYARD: How can you say that? Hitler is the creation of the capitalist class.

VON BERG [*in terrible mourning and anxiety*]: But they adore him! My own cook, my gardeners, the people who work in my forests, the chauffeur, the gamekeeper – they are *Nazis*! I saw it coming over them, the love for this creature – my housekeeper dreams of him in her bed, she'd serve my breakfast like a god had slept with her; in a dream slicing my toast! I saw this adoration in my own house! That, that is the dreadful fact. [*Controlling himself*] I beg your pardon, but it disturbs me. I admire your faith; all faith to some degree is beautiful. And when I know that yours is based on something so untrue – it's terribly disturbing. [*Quietly*] In any case, I cannot glory in the facts; there is no reassurance there. They adore him, the salt of the earth. . . . [*Staring*] Adore him.

[*There is a burst of laughter from within the office. He glances there, as they all do.*]

Strange; if I did not know that some of them in there were French, I'd have said they laugh like Germans. I suppose vulgarity has no nation, after all.

[*The door opens.* MR FERRAND *comes out, laughing; within, the laughter is subsiding. He waves within, closing the door. His smile drops. And as he goes past the* WAITER, *he glances back at the door, then quickly leans over and whispers hurriedly into his ear. They all watch. Now* FERRAND *starts away. The* WAITER *reaches out and grasps his apron.*]

WAITER: Ferrand!

FERRAND [*brushing the* WAITER'S *hand off his apron*]: What can I do? I told you fifty times to get out of this city! Didn't I? [*Starting to weep*] Didn't I?

[*He hurries up the corridor, wiping his tears with his apron. They all watch the* WAITER, *who sits there staring.*]

BAYARD: What? Tell me. Come on, I'm next, what'd he say?

WAITER [*whispers, staring ahead in shock*]: It's not to work.

LEDUC [*leaning over towards him to hear*]: What?

WAITER: They have furnaces.

BAYARD: What furnaces? . . . Talk! What is it?

WAITER: He heard the detectives; they came in for coffee just before. People get burned up in furnaces. It's not to work. They burn you up in Poland.

[*Silence. A long moment passes.*]

MONCEAU: That is the most fantastic idiocy I ever heard in my life!

LEBEAU [*to the* WAITER]: As long as you have regular French papers, though. . . . There's nothing about Jew on *my* papers.

WAITER [*in a loud whisper*]: They're going to look at your penis.

[*The* BOY *stands up as though with an electric shock. The door of the office opens; the* POLICE CAPTAIN *appears and beckons to* BAYARD. *The* BOY *quickly sits.*]

CAPTAIN: You can come now.

[BAYARD *stands, assuming an artificial and almost absurd posture of confidence. But approaching the* CAPTAIN *he achieves an authority.*]

BAYARD: I'm a master electrician with the railroad, Captain. You may have seen me there. I'm classified First Priority War Worker.

CAPTAIN: Inside.

BAYARD: You can check with Transport Minister Duquesne.

CAPTAIN: You telling me my business?

BAYARD: No, but we can all use advice from time to time.

CAPTAIN: Inside.

BAYARD: Right.

[*Without hesitation* BAYARD *walks into the office, the* CAPTAIN *following and closing the door.*

A long silence. MONCEAU, *after a moment, smooths out a rough place on the felt of his hat.* LEBEAU *looks at his papers, slowly rubbing his beard with the back of his hand, staring in terror. The* OLD JEW *draws his bundle deeper under his feet.* LEDUC *takes out a nearly empty pack of cigarettes, starts to take one for himself, then silently stands, crosses the line of men, and offers it to them.* LEBEAU *takes one.*]

They light up. Faintly, from the next-door building, an accordion is heard playing a popular tune.]

LEBEAU: Leave it to a cop to play now.

WAITER: No, that's the boss's son, Maurice. They're starting to serve lunch.

[LEDUC, *who has returned to his position as the last man on the bench, cranes around the corner of the corridor, observes, and sits back.*]

LEDUC [*quietly*]: There's only one guard at the door. Three men could take him.

[*Pause. No one responds. Then . . .*]

VON BERG [*apologetically*]: I'm afraid I'd only get in your way. I have no strength in my hands.

MONCEAU [*to* LEDUC]: You actually believe that, Doctor? About the furnaces?

LEDUC [*he thinks; then*]: I believe it is possible, yes. Come, we can do something.

MONCEAU: But what good are dead Jews to them? They want free labour. It's senseless. You can say whatever you like, but the Germans are not illogical; there's no conceivable advantage for them in such a thing.

LEDUC: You can be sitting here and still speak of advantages? Is there a rational explanation for your sitting here? But you are sitting here, aren't you?

MONCEAU: But an atrocity like that is . . . beyond any belief.

VON BERG: That is exactly the point.

MONCEAU: *You* don't believe it. Prince, you can't tell me you believe such a thing.

VON BERG: I find it the most believable atrocity I have heard.

LEBEAU: But why?

[*Slight pause.*]

VON BERG: Because it *is* so inconceivably vile. That is their power. To do the inconceivable; it paralyses the rest of us. But if that is its purpose it is not the cause. Many times I used to ask my friends – if you love your country why is it necessary to hate other countries? To be a good German why must you despise everything that is not German? Until I realized the answer. They do these things not because they are German but because they are nothing. It is the hallmark of the age – the less you exist the more important it is to make a clear impression. I can see them discussing it as a kind of . . . truthfulness. After all, what *is* self-restraint but hypocrisy? If you despise Jews the most honest thing is to burn them up. And the fact that it costs money, and uses up trains and personnel – this only guarantees the integrity, the purity, the existence of their feelings. They would even tell you that only a Jew would think of the cost. They are poets, they are striving for a new nobility, the nobility of the totally vulgar. I believe in this fire; it would prove for all time that they exist, yes, and that they were sincere. You must not calculate these people with some nineteenth-century arithmetic of loss and gain. Their motives are musi-cal, and people are merely sounds they play. And in my opinion, win or lose this war, they have pointed the way to the future. What one used to conceive a human being to be will have no room on this earth. I would try anything to get out.

[*A pause.*]

MONCEAU: But they arrested you. That German professor is an expert. There is nothing Jewish about you. . . .

VON BERG: I have an accent. I noticed he reacted when I started to speak. It is an Austrian inflexion. He may think I am another refugee.

[*The door opens. The* PROFESSOR *comes out, and indicates the* WAITER.]

PROFESSOR: Next. You.

[*The* WAITER *makes himself small, pressing up against* LEBEAU.]

Don't be alarmed, it's only to check your papers.

[*The* WAITER *suddenly bends over and runs away – around the corner and up the corridor. The* GUARD *appears at the end, col-lars him, and walks him back down the corridor.*]

WAITER [*to the* GUARD]: Felix, you know me. Felix, my wife will go crazy. Felix . . .

PROFESSOR: Take him in the office.

[*The* POLICE CAPTAIN *appears in the office doorway.*]

GUARD: There's nobody at the door.

CAPTAIN [*grabs the* WAITER *from the* GUARD]: Get in here, you Jew son-of-a-bitch. . . .

[*He throws the* WAITER *into the office; the* WAITER *collides with the* MAJOR, *who is just coming out to see what the disturbance is. The* MAJOR *grips his thigh in pain, pushing the* WAITER *clear. The* WAITER *slides to the* MAJOR'S *feet, weeping pleadingly. The* CAPTAIN *strides over and violently jerks him to his feet and pushes him into the office, going in after him.*

From within, unseen:]

You want trouble? You want trouble?

[*The* WAITER *is heard crying out; there is the sound of blows struck. Quiet. The* PROFESSOR *starts towards the door. The* MAJOR *takes his arm and leads him down to the extreme forward edge of the stage, out of hearing of the prisoners.*]

MAJOR: Wouldn't it be much simpler if they were just asked whether they . . .

[*Impatiently, without replying, the* PROFESSOR *goes over to the line of prisoners.*]

PROFESSOR: Will any of you admit right now that you are carrying forged identification papers? [*Silence.*] So. In short, you are all bona fide Frenchmen. [*Silence. He goes over to the* OLD JEW, *bends into his face.*] Are there any Jews among you? [*Silence. Then he returns to the* MAJOR.] There's the problem, Major; either we go house by house investigating everyone's biography, or we make this inspection.

MAJOR: That electrician fellow just now, though – I thought he made a point there. In fact, only this morning in the hospital, while I was waiting my turn for X-ray, another officer, a German officer, a captain, in fact – his bathrobe happened to fall open . . .

PROFESSOR: It is entirely possible.

MAJOR: It was unmistakable, Professor.

PROFESSOR: Let us be clear, Major; the Race Institute does not claim that circumcision is conclusive proof of Jewish blood. The Race Institute recognizes that a small proportion of gentiles . . .

MAJOR: I don't see any reason not to say it, Professor – I happen to be, myself.

PROFESSOR: Very well, but I certainly would never mistake you for a Jew. Any more than you could mistake a pig for a horse. Science is not capricious, Major; my degree is in racial anthropology. In any case, we can certainly separate the gentiles by this kind of examination. [*He has taken the* MAJOR'S *arm to lead him back to the office.*]

MAJOR: Excuse me. I'll be back in a few minutes. [*Moving to leave*] You can carry on without me.

PROFESSOR: Major; you have your orders; you are in command of this operation. I must insist you take your place beside me.

MAJOR: I think some mistake has been made. I am a line officer, I have no experience with things of this kind. My training is engineering and artillery.

[*Slight pause.*]

PROFESSOR [*he speaks more quietly, his eyes ablaze*]: We'd better be candid, Major. Are you refusing this assignment?

MAJOR [*registering the threat he feels*]: I'm in pain today, Professor. They are still removing fragments. In fact, I understood I was only to . . . hold this desk down until an S.S. officer took over. I'm more or less on loan, you see, from the regular Army.

PROFESSOR [*takes his arm, draws him down to the edge of the stage again*]: But the Army is not exempt from carrying out the Racial Programme. My orders come from the top. And my report will go to the top. You understand me.

MAJOR [*his resistance seems to fall*]: I do, yes.

PROFESSOR: Look now, if you wish to be relieved, I can easily telephone General von—

MAJOR: No – no, that's all right. I . . . I'll be back in a few minutes.

PROFESSOR: This is bizarre, Major – how long am I supposed to wait for you?

MAJOR [*holding back an outburst of resentment*]: I need a walk. I am not used to sitting in an office. I see nothing bizarre in it, I am a line officer, and this kind of business takes a little getting used to. [*Through his teeth*] What do you find bizarre in it?

PROFESSOR: Very well.

[*Slight pause.*]

MAJOR: I'll be back in ten minutes. You can carry on.

PROFESSOR: I will not continue without you, Major. The Army's responsibility is quite as great as mine here.

MAJOR: I won't be long.

[*The* PROFESSOR *turns abruptly and strides into the office, slamming the door shut. Very much wanting to get out, the* MAJOR *goes up the corridor.* LEDUC *stands as he passes.*]

LEDUC: Major . . .

[*The* MAJOR *limps past him without turning, up the corridor and out. Silence.*]

BOY: Mister?

[LEDUC *turns to him.*]

I'd try it with you.

LEDUC [*to* MONCEAU *and* LEBEAU]: What about you two?

LEBEAU: Whatever you say, but I'm so hungry I wouldn't do you much good.

LEDUC: You can walk up to him and start an argument. Distract his attention. Then we—

MONCEAU: You're both crazy, they'll shoot you down.

LEDUC: Some of us might make it. There's only one man at the door. This neighbourhood is full of alleyways – you could disappear in twenty yards.

MONCEAU: How long would you be free – an hour? And when they catch you they'll really tear you apart.

BOY: Please! I have to get out. I was on my way to the pawn-shop. [*Takes out a ring.*] It's my mother's wedding ring, it's all that's left. She's waiting for the money. They have nothing in the house to eat.

MONCEAU: You take my advice, boy; don't do anything, they'll let you go.

LEDUC: Like the electrician?

MONCEAU: He was obviously a Communist. And the waiter irritated the Captain.

LEBEAU: Look, I'll try it with you but don't expect too much; I'm weak as a chicken, I haven't eaten since yesterday.

LEDUC [*to* MONCEAU]: It would be better with another man.

The boy is very light. If you and the boy rush him I'll get his gun away.

VON BERG [*to* LEDUC, *looking at his hands*]: Forgive me.

[MONCEAU *springs up, goes to a box, and sits.*]

MONCEAU: I am not going to risk my life for nothing. That businessman had a Jewish face. [*To* LEBEAU] You said so yourself.

LEBEAU [*to* LEDUC, *appeasingly*]: I did. I thought so. Look, if your papers are good, maybe that's it.

LEDUC [*to* LEBEAU *and* MONCEAU]: You know yourself the Germans have been moving into the Southern Zone; you see they are picking up Jews; a man has just told you that you are marked for destruction. . . .

MONCEAU [*indicates* VON BERG]: They took him in. Nobody's explained it.

VON BERG: My accent . . .

MONCEAU: My dear Prince, only an idiot could mistake you for anything but an Austrian of the upper class. I took you for nobility the minute you walked in.

LEDUC: But if it's a general check-up why would they be looking at penises?

MONCEAU: There's no evidence of that!

LEDUC: The waiter's boss . . .

MONCEAU [*suppressing a nervous shout*]: He overheard two French detectives who can't possibly know anything about what happens in Poland. And if they do that kind of thing, it's not the end either – I had Jew stamped on my passport in Paris and I was playing Cyrano at the same time.

VON BERG: Really! Cyrano!

LEBEAU: Then why'd you leave Paris?

MONCEAU: It was an absolutely idiotic accident. I was rooming with another actor, a gentile. And he kept warning me to get out. But naturally one doesn't just give up a role like that. But one night I let myself be influenced by him. He pointed out that I had a number of books which were on the forbidden list – of Communist literature – I mean things like Sinclair Lewis, and Thomas Mann, and even a few things by Friedrich Engels, which everybody was reading at one time. And I decided I might as well get rid of them. So we made bundles and I lived on the fifth floor of a walk-up and we'd take turns going down to the street and just leaving them on benches or in doorways or anywhere at all. It was after midnight, and I was just dropping a bundle into the gutter near the Opera, when I noticed a man standing in a doorway watching me. At that moment I realized that I had stamped my name and address in every one of those books.

VON BERG: Hah! What did you do?

MONCEAU: Started walking, and kept right on down here to the Unoccupied Zone. [*An outcry of remorse*] But in my opinion, if I'd done nothing at all I might still be working!

LEDUC [*with higher urgency, but deeply sympathetic; to* MONCEAU]: Listen to me for one moment. I beg you. There is only one man guarding that door; we may never get another chance like this again.

LEBEAU: That's another thing; if it was all that serious, wouldn't they be guarding us more heavily? I mean, that's a point.

LEDUC: That is exactly the point. They are relying on us.

MONCEAU: Relying on us!

LEDUC: Yes. To project our own reasonable ideas into their heads. It is reasonable that a light guard means the thing is not important. They rely on our own logic to immobilize ourselves. But you have just told us how you went all over Paris advertising the fact that you owned forbidden books.

MONCEAU: But I didn't do it purposely.

LEDUC: May I guess that you could no longer bear the tension of remaining in Paris? But that you wanted to keep your role in Cyrano and had to find some absolute compulsion to save your own life? It was your unconscious mind that saved you. Do you understand? You cannot wager your life on a purely rational analysis of this situation. Listen to your feelings; you must certainly *feel* the danger here. . . .

MONCEAU [*in high anxiety*]: I played in Germany. That audience could not burn up actors in a furnace. [*Turning to* VON BERG] Prince, you cannot tell me you believe that!

VON BERG [*after a pause*]: I supported a small orchestra. When the Germans came into Austria three of the players prepared to escape. I convinced them no harm would come to them; I brought them to my castle; we all lived together. The oboist was twenty, twenty-one – the heart stopped when he played certain tones. They came for him in the garden. They took him out of his chair. The instrument lay on the lawn like a dead bone. I made certain inquiries; he is dead now. And it was even more terrible – they came and sat down and listened until the rehearsal was over. And *then* they took him. It is as though they wished to take him at exactly the moment when he was most beautiful. I know how you feel – but I tell you nothing any longer is forbidden. Nothing. [*Tears are in his eyes; he turns to* LEDUC.] I ask you to forgive me, Doctor.

[*Pause.*]

BOY: Will they let you go?

VON BERG [*with a guilty glance at the* BOY]: I suppose. If this is all to catch Jews they will let me go.

BOY: Would you take this ring? And bring it back to my mother?

[*He stretches his hand out with the ring.* VON BERG *does not touch it.*]

Number nine Rue Charlot. Top floor. Hirsch. Sarah Hirsch. She has long brown hair . . . be sure it's her. She has a little beauty mark on this cheek. There are two other families in the apartment, so be sure it's her.

[VON BERG *looks into the* BOY'S *face. Silence. Then he turns to* LEDUC.]

VON BERG: Come. Tell me what to do. I'll try to help you. [*To* LEDUC] Doctor?

LEDUC: I'm afraid it's hopeless.

VON BERG: Why?

LEDUC [*stares ahead, then looks at* LEBEAU]: He's weak with hunger, and the boy's like a feather. I wanted to get away, not just be slaughtered. [*Pause. With bitter irony*] I live in the country, you see; I haven't talked to anybody in so long, I'm afraid I came in here with the wrong assumptions.

MONCEAU: If you're trying to bait me, Doctor, forget it.

LEDUC: Would you mind telling me, are you religious?

MONCEAU: Not at all.

LEDUC: Then why do you feel this desire to be sacrificed?

MONCEAU: I ask you to stop talking to me.

LEDUC: But you are making a gift of yourself. You are the only able-bodied man here, aside from me, and yet you feel no impulse to do something? I don't understand your air of confidence.

[*Pause.*]

MONCEAU: I refuse to play a part I do not fit. Everyone is playing the victim these days; hopeless, hysterical, they always assume the worst. I have papers; I will present them with the single idea that they must be honoured. I think that is exactly what saved that businessman. You accuse us of acting the part the Germans created for us; I think you're the one who's doing that by acting so desperate.

LEDUC: And if, despite your act, they throw you into a freight car?

MONCEAU: I don't think they will.

LEDUC: But if they do. You certainly have enough imagination to visualize that.

MONCEAU: In that case, I will have done my best. I know what failure is; it took me a long time to make good; I haven't the personality for leading roles; everyone said I was crazy to stay in the profession. But I did, and I imposed my idea on others.

LEDUC: In other words, you will create yourself.

MONCEAU: Every actor creates himself.

LEDUC: But when they tell you to open your fly.

[MONCEAU *is silent, furious.*]

Please don't stop now; I'm very interested. How do you regard that moment?

[MONCEAU *is silent.*]

Believe me, I am only trying to understand this. I am incapable of penetrating such passivity; I ask you what is in your mind when you face the command to open your fly. I am being as impersonal, as scientific as I know how to be – I believe I am going to be murdered. What do you believe will happen when they point to that spot between your legs?

[*Pause.*]

MONCEAU: I have nothing to say to you.

LEBEAU: I'll tell you what I'll feel. [*Indicates* VON BERG.] I'll wish I was him.

LEDUC: To be someone else.

LEBEAU [*exhausted*]: Yes. To have been arrested by mistake. God – to see them relaxing when they realize I am innocent.

LEDUC: You feel guilty, then.

LEBEAU [*he has gradually become closer to exhaustion*]: A little, I guess. Not for anything I've done but . . . I don't know why.

LEDUC: For being a Jew, perhaps?

LEBEAU: I'm not ashamed of being a Jew.

LEDUC: Then why feel guilty?

LEBEAU: I don't know. Maybe it's that they keep saying such terrible things about us, and you can't answer. And after years and years of it, you . . . I wouldn't say you believe it, but . . . you do, a little. It's a funny thing – I used to say to my mother and father just what you're saying. We could have gone to America a month before the invasion. But they wouldn't leave Paris. She had this brass bed, and carpets, and draperies and all kinds of junk. Like him with his Cyrano. And I told them, 'You're doing just what they want you to do!' But, see, people won't believe they can be killed. Not them with their brass bed and their carpets and their faces. . . .

LEDUC: But do you believe it? It seems to me you don't believe it yourself.

LEBEAU: I believe it. They only caught me this morning because I . . . I always used to walk in the morning before I sat down to work. And I wanted to do it again. I knew I shouldn't go outside. But you get tired of believing in the truth. You get tired of seeing things clearly. [*Pause.*] I always collected my illusions in the morning. I could never paint what I saw, only what I imagined. And this morning, danger or no danger, I just had to get out, to walk around, to see something real, something else but the inside of my head . . . and I hardly turned the corner and that motherless son-of-a bitch of a scientist got out of the car with his fingers going for my nose. . . . [*Pause.*] I believe I can die. But you can get so tired . . .

LEDUC: That it's not too bad.

LEBEAU: Almost, yes.

LEDUC [*glancing at them all*]: So that one way or the other, with illusions or without them, exhausted or fresh – we have been trained to die. The Jew and the gentile both.

MONCEAU: You're still trying to bait me, Doctor, but if you want to commit suicide do it alone, don't involve others. The fact is there are laws and every government enforces its laws; and I want it understood that I have nothing to do with any of this talk.

LEDUC [*angering now*]: Every government does not have laws condemning people because of their race.

MONCEAU: I beg your pardon. The Russians condemn the middle class, the English have condemned the Indians, Africans, and anybody else they could lay their hands on, the French, the Italians . . . every nation has condemned somebody because of his race, including the Americans and what they do to Negroes. The vast majority of mankind is condemned because of its race. What do you advise all these people – suicide?

LEDUC: What do you advise?

MONCEAU [*seeking and finding conviction*]: I go on the assumption that if I obey the law with dignity I will live in peace. I may not like the law, but evidently the majority does, or they would overthrow it. And I'm speaking now of the French majority, who outnumber the Germans in this town fifty to one. These are French police, don't forget, not German. And if by some miracle you did knock out that guard you would find yourself in a city where not one person in a thousand would help you. And it's got nothing to do with being Jewish or not Jewish. It is what the world is, so why don't you stop insulting others with romantic challenges!

LEDUC: In short, because the world is indifferent you will wait calmly and with great dignity – to open your fly.

MONCEAU [*frightened and furious, he stands*]: I'll tell you what I think; I think it's people like you who brought this on us. People who give Jews a reputation for subversion, and this Talmudic analysis, and this everlasting, niggling discontent.

LEDUC: Then I will tell you that I was wrong before; you

didn't advertise your name on those forbidden books in order to find a reason to leave Paris and save yourself. It was in order to get yourself caught and be put out of your misery. Your heart is conquered territory, mister.

MONCEAU: If we meet again you will pay for that remark.

LEDUC: Conquered territory! [*He leans forward, his head in his hands.*]

BOY [*reaching over to hand the ring to* VON BERG]: Will you do it? Number nine Rue Charlot?

VON BERG [*deeply affected*]: I will try.

[*He takes the ring. The* BOY *immediately stands.*]

LEDUC: Where are you going?

[*The* BOY, *terrified but desperate, moves on the balls of his feet to the corridor and peeks around the corner.* LEDUC *stands, tries to draw him back.*]

You can't; it'll take three men to . . .

[*The* BOY *shakes loose and walks rapidly up the hallway.* LEDUC *hesitates, then goes after him.*]

Wait! Wait a minute! I'm coming.

[*The* MAJOR *enters the corridor at its far end. The* BOY *halts,* LEDUC *now beside him. For a moment they stand facing him. Then they turn and come down the corridor and sit, the* MAJOR *following them. He touches* LEDUC'S *sleeves, and* LEDUC *stands and follows him downstage.*]

MAJOR [*he is 'high' – with drink and a flow of emotion*]: That's impossible. Don't try it. There are sentries on both corners. [*Glancing towards the office door*] Captain, I would only like to say that . . . this is all as inconceivable to me as it is to you. Can you believe that?

LEDUC: I'd believe it if you shot yourself. And better yet, if you took a few of them with you.

MAJOR [*wiping his mouth with the back of his hand*]: We would all be replaced by tomorrow morning, wouldn't we?

LEDUC: We might get out alive, though; you could see to that.

MAJOR: They'd find you soon.

LEDUC: Not me.

MAJOR [*with a manic amusement, yet deeply questioning*]: Why do you deserve to live more than I do?

LEDUC: Because I am incapable of doing what you are doing. I am better for the world than you.

MAJOR: It means nothing to you that I have feelings about this?

LEDUC: Nothing whatever, unless you get us out of here.

MAJOR: And then what? Then what?

LEDUC: I will remember a decent German, an honourable German.

MAJOR: Will that make a difference?

LEDUC: I will love you as long as I live. Will anyone do that now?

MAJOR: That means so much to you – that someone love you?

LEDUC: That I be worthy of someone's love, yes. And respect.

MAJOR: It's amazing; you don't understand anything. Nothing of that kind is left, don't you understand that yet?

LEDUC: It is left in me.

MAJOR [*more loudly, a fury rising in him*]: There are no persons any more, don't you see that? There will never be persons again. What do I care if you love me? Are you out of your mind? What am I, a dog that I must be loved? You [*turning to all of them*] goddamned Jews!

[*The door opens; the* PROFESSOR *and the* POLICE CAPTAIN *appear.*]

Like dogs, Jew-dogs. Look at him [*indicating the* OLD JEW] with his paws folded. Look what happens when I yell at him. Dog! He doesn't move. Does he move? Do you see him moving? [*He strides to the* PROFESSOR *and takes him by the arm.*] But we move, don't we? We measure your noses, don't we, Herr Professor, and we look at your cocks, we keep moving continually!

PROFESSOR [*with a gesture to draw him inside*]: Major . . .

MAJOR: Hands off, you civilian bastard.

PROFESSOR: I think . . .

MAJOR [*drawing his revolver*]: Not a word!

PROFESSOR: You're drunk.

[*The* MAJOR *fires into the ceiling. The prisoners tense in shock.*]

MAJOR: Everything stops now. [*He goes in thought, revolver cocked in his hand, and sits beside* LEBEAU.] Now it is all stopped.

[*His hands are shaking. He sniffs in his running nose. He crosses his legs to control them, and looks at* LEDUC, *who is still standing.*] Now you tell me. You tell me. Now nothing is moving. You tell me. Go ahead now.

LEDUC: What shall I tell you?

MAJOR: Tell me how . . . how there can be persons any more. I have you at the end of this revolver [*indicates the* PROFESSOR] he has me – and somebody has him – and somebody has somebody else. Now tell me.

LEDUC: I told you.

MAJOR: I won't repeat it. I am a man of honour. What do you make of that? I will not tell them what you advised me to do. What do you say – damned decent of me, isn't it . . . not to repeat your advice?

[LEDUC *is silent. The* MAJOR *gets up, comes to* LEDUC. *Pause.*]

You are a combat veteran.

LEDUC: Yes.

MAJOR: No record of subversive activities against the German authority.

LEDUC: No.

MAJOR: If you were released, and the others were kept . . . would you refuse?

[LEDUC *starts to turn away. The* MAJOR *nudges him with the pistol, forcing him face to face.*]

Would you refuse?

LEDUC: No.

MAJOR: And walk out of that door with a light heart?

LEDUC [*he is looking at the floor now*]: I don't know. [*He starts to put his trembling hands into his pockets.*]

MAJOR: Don't hide your hands. I am trying to understand why you are better for the world than me. Why do you hide your hands? Would you go out that door with a light heart, run to your woman, drink a toast to your skin? . . . Why are you better than anybody else?

LEDUC: I have no duty to make a gift of myself to your sadism.

MAJOR: But I do? To others' sadism? Of myself? I have that duty and you do not? To make a gift of myself?

LEDUC [*looks at the* PROFESSOR *and the* POLICE CAPTAIN, *glances back at the* MAJOR]: I have nothing to say.

MAJOR: That's better. [*He suddenly gives* LEDUC *an almost comradely push and nearly laughs. He puts his gun away, turns swaying to the* PROFESSOR *and with a victorious shout*] Next! [*The* MAJOR *brushes past the* PROFESSOR *into the office.* LEBEAU *has not moved.*]

PROFESSOR: This way.

[LEBEAU *stands up, starts sleepily towards the corridor, turns about, and moves into the office, the* PROFESSOR *following him.*]

CAPTAIN [*to* LEDUC]: Get back there.

[LEDUC *returns to his seat. The* CAPTAIN *goes into the office; the door shuts. Pause.*]

MONCEAU: You happy now? You got him furious. You happy?

[*The door opens; the* CAPTAIN *appears, beckoning to* MONCEAU.]

CAPTAIN: Next.

[MONCEAU *gets up at once; taking papers out of his jacket, he fixes a smile on his face and walks with erect elegance to the* CAPTAIN *and with a slight bow, his voice cheerful*]

MONCEAU: Good morning, Captain.

[*He goes right into the office; the* CAPTAIN *follows, and shuts the door. Pause.*]

BOY: Number nine Rue Charlot. Please.

VON BERG: I'll give it to her.

BOY: I'm a minor. I'm not even fifteen. Does it apply to minors?

[CAPTAIN *opens the door, beckons to the* BOY.]

BOY [*standing*]: I'm a minor. I'm not fifteen until February . . .

CAPTAIN: Inside.

BOY [*halting before the* CAPTAIN]: I could get my birth certificate for you.

CAPTAIN [*prodding him along*]: Inside, inside.

[*They go in. The door shuts. The accordion is heard again from next door. The* OLD JEW *begins to rock back and forth slightly, praying softly.* VON BERG, *his hand trembling as it passes down his cheek, stares at the* OLD JEW, *then turns to* LEDUC *on his other side. The three are alone now.*]

VON BERG: Does he realize what is happening?

LEDUC [*with an edgy note of impatience*]: As much as anyone can, I suppose.

VON BERG: He seems to be watching it all from the stars. [*Slight pause.*] I wish we could have met under other circumstances. There are a great many things I'd like to have asked you.

LEDUC [*rapidly, sensing the imminent summons*]: I'd appreciate it if you'd do me a favour.

VON BERG: Certainly.

LEDUC: Will you go and tell my wife?

VON BERG: Where is she?

LEDUC: Take the main highway north two kilometres. You'll see a small forest on the left and a dirt road leading into it. Go about a kilometre until you see the river. Follow the river to a small mill. They are in the tool shed behind the wheel.

VON BERG [*distressed*]: And . . . what shall I say?

LEDUC: That I've been arrested. And that there may be a possibility I can . . . [*Breaks off.*] No, tell her the truth.

VON BERG [*alarmed*]: What do you mean?

LEDUC: The furnaces. Tell her that.

VON BERG: But actually . . . that's only a rumour, isn't it?

LEDUC [*turns to him – sharply*]: I don't regard it as a rumour. It should be known. I never heard of it before. It must be known. Just take her aside – there's no need for the children to hear it, but tell her.

VON BERG: It's only that it would be difficult for me. To tell such a thing to a woman.

LEDUC: If it's happening you can find a way to say it, can't you?

VON BERG [*hesitates; he senses* LEDUC'S *resentment*]: Very well. I'll tell her. It's only that I have no great . . . facility with women. But I'll do as you say. [*Pause. He glances to the door.*] They're taking longer with that boy. Maybe he *is* too young, you suppose?

[LEDUC *does not answer.* VON BERG *seems suddenly hopeful.*]
They would stick to the rules, you know. . . . In fact, with

the shortage of physicians you suppose they– [*He breaks off.*]
I'm sorry if I said anything to offend you.

LEDUC [*struggling with his anger*]: That's all right. [*Slight pause.
His voice is trembling with anger.*] It's just that you keep finding
these little shreds of hope and it's a little difficult.

VON BERG: Yes, I see. I beg your pardon. I understand.
[*Pause.* LEDUC *glances at the door; he is shifting about in high
tension.*]
Would you like to talk of something else, perhaps? Are you
interested in . . . in music?

LEDUC [*desperately trying to control himself*]: It's really quite
simple. It's that you'll survive, you see.

VON BERG: But I can't help that, can I?

LEDUC: That only makes it worse! I'm sorry, one isn't always
in control of one's emotions.

VON BERG: Doctor, I can promise you – it will not be easy
for me to walk out of here. You don't know me.

LEDUC [*he tries not to reply; then*]: I'm afraid it will only be
difficult because it is so easy.

VON BERG: I think that's unfair.

LEDUC: Well, it doesn't matter.

VON BERG: It does to me. I . . . I can tell you that I was very
close to suicide in Austria. Actually, that is why I left. When
they murdered my musicians – not that alone, but when I
told the story to many of my friends there was hardly any
reaction. That was almost worse. Do you understand such
indifference?

LEDUC [*he seems on the verge of an outbreak*]: You have a curious
idea of human nature. It's astounding you can go on with it
in these times.

VON BERG [*with hand on heart*]: But what is left if one gives up
one's ideals? What *is* there?

LEDUC: Who are you talking about? You? Or me?

VON BERG: I'm terribly sorry. . . . I understand.

LEDUC: Why don't you just stop talking. I can't listen to
anything. [*Slight pause.*] Forgive me. I do appreciate your
feeling. [*Slight pause.*] I see it too clearly, perhaps – I know
the violence inside these people's heads. It's difficult to
listen to amelioration, even if it's well meant.

VON BERG: I had no intention of ameliorating—

LEDUC: I think you do. And you must; you will survive, you will have to ameliorate it; just a little, just enough. It's no reflection on you. [*Slight pause.*] But, you see, this is why one gets so furious. Because all this suffering is so pointless – it can never be a lesson, it can never have a meaning. And that is why it will be repeated again and again for ever.

VON BERG: Because it cannot be shared?

LEDUC: Yes. Because it cannot be shared. It is total, absolute, waste. [*He leans forward suddenly, trying to collect himself against his terror. He glances at the door.*] How strange – one can even become impatient. [*A groan as he shakes his head with wonder and anger at himself.*] Hm! – what devils they are.

VON BERG [*with an overtone of closeness to* LEDUC]: You understand now why I left Vienna. They can make death seductive. It is their worst sin. I had dreams at night – Hitler in a great flowing cloak, almost like a gown, almost like a woman. He was beautiful.

LEDUC: Listen – don't mention the furnaces to my wife.

VON BERG: I'm glad you say that, I feel very relieved, there's really no point . . .

LEDUC [*in a higher agony as he realizes*]: No, it's . . . it's. . . . You see there was no reason for me to be caught here. We have a good hideout. They'd never have found us. But she has an exposed nerve in one tooth and I thought I might find some codeine. Just say I was arrested.

VON BERG: Does she have sufficient money?

LEDUC: You could help her that way if you like. Thank you.

VON BERG: The children are small?

LEDUC: Two and three.

VON BERG: How dreadful. How dreadful. [*He looks with a glance of fury at the door.*] Do you suppose if I offered him something? I can get hold of a good deal of money. I know so little about people – I'm afraid he's rather an idealist. It could infuriate him more.

LEDUC: You might try to feel him out. I don't know what to tell you.

VON BERG: How upside down everything is – to find oneself wishing for a money-loving cynic!

LEDUC: It's perfectly natural. We have learned the price of idealism.

VON BERG: And yet can one wish for a world without ideals? That's what's so depressing – one doesn't know what to wish for.

LEDUC [*in anger*]: You see, I knew it when I walked down the road. I knew it was senseless! For a goddamned toothache! So what, so she doesn't sleep for a couple of weeks! It was perfectly clear I shouldn't be taking the chance.

VON BERG: Yes, but if one loves someone . . .

LEDUC: We are not in love any more. It's just too difficult to separate in these times.

VON BERG: Oh, how terrible.

LEDUC [*more softly, realizing a new idea*]: Listen . . . about the furnaces . . . don't mention that to her. Not a word, please. [*With great self-contempt*] God, at a time like this – to think of taking vengeance on her! What scum we are! [*He almost sways in despair.*]

[*Pause.* VON BERG *turns to* LEDUC; *tears are in his eyes.*]

VON BERG: There is nothing, is that it? For you there is nothing?

LEDUC [*flying out at him suddenly*]: Well what do you propose? Excuse me, but what in hell are you talking about?

[*The door opens. The* PROFESSOR *comes out and beckons to the* OLD JEW. *He seems upset, by an argument he had in the office, possibly.*]

Next.

[*The* OLD JEW *does not turn to him.*]

You hear me, why do you sit there?

[*He strides to the* OLD JEW *and lifts him to his feet brusquely. The man reaches down to pick up his bundle, but the* PROFESSOR *tries to push it back to the floor.*]

Leave that.

[*With a wordless little cry, the* OLD JEW *clings to his bundle.*]

Leave it!

[*The* PROFESSOR *strikes at the* OLD JEW'S *hand, but he only holds on tighter, uttering his wordless little cries. The* POLICE CAPTAIN *comes out as the* PROFESSOR *pulls at the bundle.*]

Let go of that!

[*The bundle rips open. A white cloud of feathers blows up out of it. For an instant everything stops as the* PROFESSOR *looks in surprise at the feathers floating down. The* MAJOR *appears in the doorway as the feathers settle.*]

CAPTAIN: Come on.

[*The* CAPTAIN *and the* PROFESSOR *lift the* OLD JEW *and carry him past the* MAJOR *into the office. The* MAJOR *with deadened eyes glances at the feathers and limps in, closing the door behind him.*

LEDUC *and* VON BERG *stare at the feathers, some of which have fallen on them. They silently brush them off.* LEDUC *picks the last one off his jacket, opens his fingers, and lets it fall to the floor.*

Silence. Suddenly a short burst of laughter is heard from the office.]

VON BERG [*with great difficulty, not looking at* LEDUC]: I would like to be able to part with your friendship. Is that possible?
[*Pause.*]

LEDUC: Prince, in my profession one gets the habit of looking at oneself quite impersonally. It is not you I am angry with. In one part of my mind it is not even this Nazi. I am only angry that I should have been born before the day when man has accepted his own nature; that he is *not* reasonable, that he is full of murder, that his ideals are only the little tax he pays for the right to hate and kill with a clear conscience. I am only angry that, knowing this, I still deluded myself. That there was not time to truly make part of myself what I know, and to teach others the truth.

VON BERG [*angered, above his anxiety*]: There are ideals, Doctor, of another kind. There are people who would find it easier to die than stain one finger with this murder. They exist. I swear it to you. People for whom everything is *not* permitted, foolish people and ineffectual, but they do exist and will not dishonour their tradition. [*Desperately*] I ask your friendship.

[*Again laughter is heard from within the office. This time it is louder.* LEDUC *slowly turns to* VON BERG.]

LEDUC: I owe you the truth, Prince; you won't believe it now, but I wish you would think about it and what it means. I have never analysed a gentile who did not have, somewhere hidden in his mind, a dislike if not a hatred for the Jews.

VON BERG [*clapping his ears shut, springing up*]: That is impossible, it is not true of me!

LEDUC [*standing, coming to him, a wild pity in his voice*]: Until you know it is true of you you will destroy whatever truth can come of this atrocity. Part of knowing who we are is knowing we are not someone else. And Jew is only the name we give to that stranger, that agony we cannot feel, that death we look at like a cold abstraction. Each man has his Jew; it is the other. And the Jews have their Jews. And now, now above all, you must see that you have yours – the man whose death leaves you relieved that you are not him, despite your decency. And that is why there is nothing and will be nothing – until you face your own complicity with this . . . your own humanity.

VON BERG: I deny that. I deny that absolutely. I have never in my life said a word against your people. Is that your implication? That I have something to do with this monstrousness! I have put a pistol to my head! To my head!

[*Laughter is heard again.*]

LEDUC [*hopelessly*]: I'm sorry; it doesn't really matter.

VON BERG: It matters very much to me. Very much to me!

LEDUC [*in a level tone full of mourning; and yet behind it a howling horror*]: Prince, you asked me before if I knew your cousin, Baron Kessler.

[VON BERG *looks at him, already with anxiety.*]

Baron Kessler is a Nazi. He helped to remove all the Jewish doctors from the medical school.

[VON BERG *is struck; his eyes glance about.*]

You were aware of that, weren't you?

[*Half-hysterical laughter comes from the office.*]

You must have heard that at some time or another, didn't you?

VON BERG [*stunned, inward-seeing*]: Yes, I heard it. I . . . had forgotten it. You see, he was . . .

LEDUC: . . . Your cousin. I understand.

[*They are quite joined; and* LEDUC *is mourning for the* PRINCE *as much as for himself, despite his anger.*]

And in any case, it is only a small part of Baron Kessler to you. I do understand it. But it is all of Baron Kessler to me. When you said his name it was with love; and I'm sure he must be a man of some kindness, with whom you can see eye to eye in many things. But when I hear that name I see a knife. You see now why I say there is nothing, and will be nothing, when even you cannot really put yourself in my place? Even you! And that is why your thoughts of suicide do not move me. It's not your guilt I want, it's your responsibility – that might have helped. Yes, if you had understood that Baron Kessler was in part, in some part, in some small and frightful part – doing your will. You might have done something then, with your standing, and your name and your decency, aside from shooting yourself!

VON BERG [*in full horror, his face upthrust, calling*]: What can ever save us? [*He covers his face with his hands.*]

[*The door opens. The* PROFESSOR *comes out.*]

PROFESSOR [*beckoning to the* PRINCE]: Next.

[VON BERG *does not turn, but holds* LEDUC *in his horrified, beseeching gaze. The* PROFESSOR *approaches the* PRINCE.]

Come!

[*The* PROFESSOR *reaches down to take* VON BERG'S *arm.* VON BERG *angrily brushes away his abhorrent hand.*]

VON BERG: *Hände weg!*

[*The* PROFESSOR *retracts his hand, immobilized, surprised, and for a moment has no strength against his own recognition of authority.* VON BERG *turns back to* LEDUC, *who glances up at him and smiles with warmth, then turns away.*

VON BERG *turns towards the door and, reaching into his breast pocket for a wallet of papers, goes into the office. The* PROFESSOR *follows and closes the door.*

Alone, LEDUC *sits motionless. Now he begins the movements of the trapped; he swallows with difficulty, crosses and recrosses his legs. Now he is still again and bends over and cranes around the corner of the corridor to look for the* GUARD. *A movement of his foot stirs up feathers. The accordion is heard* outside. *He angrily kicks a feather off his foot. Now he makes a decision; he quickly reaches into his pocket, takes out a clasp knife, opens the blade, and begins to get to his feet, starting for the corridor.*

The door opens and VON BERG *comes out. In his hand is a white pass. The door shuts behind him. He is looking at the pass as he goes by* LEDUC, *and suddenly turns, walks back, and thrusts the pass into* LEDUC'S *hand.*]

VON BERG [*in a strangely angered whisper, motioning him out*]: Take it! Go!

[VON BERG *sits quickly on the bench, taking out the wedding ring.* LEDUC *stares at him, a horrified look on his face.* VON BERG *hands him the ring.*]

Number nine Rue Charlot. Go.

LEDUC [*in a desperate whisper*]: What will happen to you?

VON BERG [*angrily waving him away*]: Go, go!

[LEDUC *backs away, his hands springing to cover his eyes in the awareness of his own guilt.*]

LEDUC [*a plea in his voice*]: I wasn't asking you to do this! You don't owe me this!

VON BERG: Go!

[LEDUC, *his eyes wide in awe and terror suddenly turns and strides up the corridor. At the end of it the* GUARD *appears, hearing his footsteps. He gives the* GUARD *the pass and disappears.*

A long pause. The door opens. The PROFESSOR *appears.*]

PROFESSOR: Ne– [*He breaks off. Looks about, then, to* VON BERG] Where's your pass?

[VON BERG *stares ahead. The* PROFESSOR *calls into the office.*]

Man escaped! [*He runs up the corridor, calling.*] Man escaped! Man escaped!

[*The* POLICE CAPTAIN *rushes out of the office. Voices are heard outside calling orders. The accordion stops. The* MAJOR *hurries out of the office. The* POLICE CAPTAIN *rushes past him.*]

CAPTAIN: What? [*Glancing back at* VON BERG, *he realizes and rushes up the corridor, calling*] Who let him out? Find that man! What happened?

[*The voices outside are swept away by a siren going off. The* MAJOR *has gone to the opening of the corridor, following the* POLICE CAPTAIN. *For a moment he remains looking up the corridor. All that can be heard now is the siren moving off in pursuit. It dies away, leaving the* MAJOR'S *rapid and excited breaths, angry breaths, incredulous breaths.*

Now he turns slowly to VON BERG, *who is staring straight ahead.* VON BERG *turns and faces him. Then he gets to his feet. The moment lengthens and lengthens yet. A look of anguish and fury is stiffening the* MAJOR'S *face; he is closing his fists. They stand there, for ever incomprehensible to one another, looking into each other's eyes.*

At the head of the corridor four new men, prisoners, appear. Herded by the DETECTIVES, *they enter the detention room and sit on the bench, glancing about at the ceiling, the walls, the feathers on the floor, and the two men who are staring at each other so strangely.*]

CURTAIN

EDWARD ALBEE

WHO'S AFRAID OF VIRGINIA WOOLF?

'Frighteningly well-observed picture of a matrimonial *corrida*, with the scarred and bloody husband at last taking the cow by the horns after a long, liquor-logged evening' – Alan Brien in the *Sunday Telegraph*

'It has established Albee in the world's mind as the proper successor to Tennessee Williams and Arthur Miller' – Bamber Gascoigne in the *Observer*

'He is the most exciting American playwright of his generation' – *Vogue*

'Has an intensity, a demoniac misery, a ferocious humour, an ability to rend and tear and crucify to a degree unfamiliar in the English theatre . . . no one can remain indifferent to its power, its resilience of ideas and its range of language' – Harold Hobson in the *Sunday Times*

ARTHUR MILLER

DEATH OF A SALESMAN

'A salesman's got to dream, boy. It comes with the territory.' But Willy had the wrong dreams. All, all wrong.

Death of a Salesman was written in six weeks in the spring of 1948, but it had been brewing in Miller's mind for ten years. Its 742 performances put it among the 50 longest recorded Broadway runs: it received the Pulitzer Prize for Theatre and was later filmed. Miller himself defined his aim in the play as being 'to set forth what happens when a man does not have a grip on the forces of life'.

and

A VIEW FROM THE BRIDGE and ALL MY SONS
THE CRUCIBLE
AFTER THE FALL
THE PRICE

TENNESSEE WILLIAMS

CAT ON A HOT TIN ROOF
THE MILK TRAIN DOESN'T STOP HERE ANYMORE
THE NIGHT OF THE IGUANA

Tennessee Williams once wrote: 'Personal lyricism is the outcry of prisoner to prisoner from the cell in solitary where each is confined for the duration of his life.' *Cat on a Hot Tin Roof*, set in the constricted heart of the American South, is a drama of a family imprisoned in the midst of untold richness by greed, envy and crippling self-deception.

In *The Milk Train Doesn't Stop Here Anymore* an American actress has retreated to a luxurious Mediterranean hide-out, where she dictates her memoirs and fights strenuously against the incursions of illness and old age.

The Night of the Iguana was presented in New York in 1961 and later adapted for a film made by John Huston. Set in 'a rather rustic and very Bohemian hotel' on a hill-top in Mexico at the time of the Battle of Britain, the play brings together an intriguing assortment of characters: an affable and lusty hotel proprietor, a defrocked clergyman working as a tourist guide; an old poet; and a family of coarse, beer-drinking Nazis.

also published in Penguin Plays

SWEET BIRD OF YOUTH / A STREET CAR NAMED DESIRE /
THE GLASS MANAGERIE

PERIOD OF ADJUSTMENT / SUMMER AND SMOKE /
SMALL CRAFT WARNINGS

ROSE TATTOO / CAMINO REAL /
ORPHEUS DESCENDING